# The Answers to All Your Questions are in the Dice

*Donald Tyson's interpretation of the runes, and their divinatory meanings are derived from authentic sources such as the old runic poems, and hence are much closer to the ancient grain than most modern re-interpretations. I have the greatest possible respect for Mr. Tyson's work. The instructions for Rune Dice divination are as clear and well-written as possible and the section on runic magic even taught me a few bits of lore.*

—Kenneth Johnson
author of *Jaguar Wisdom*
and co-author of *Silver Wheel* & *The Grail Castle*

Gain a detailed and exact response to any question in moments. Portable, durable, and easy to read at a glance, the rune dice are the ideal method for divining the future and revealing unknown matters of the past or present. Get the answers you want and the insights you need to make the best decisions, take advantage of life's opportunities, and to navigate your way into the new millennium.

## About the Author

Donald Tyson is a Canadian from Halifax, Nova Scotia. Early in life, he was drawn to science by an intense fascination with astronomy. He began university seeking a science degree, but became disillusioned with the aridity and futility of a mechanistic view of the universe, and shifted his major to English. After graduating with honors, he has pursued a writing career.

He now devotes his life to the attainment of a complete gnosis of the art of magic in theory and practice. His purpose is to formulate an accessible system of personal training, composed of East and West, past and present, which will help the individual discover the reason for one's existence and a way to fulfill it.

## To Write to the Author

If you would like to contact the author or would like more information about this book, please write to him in care of Llewellyn Worldwide. We cannot guarantee every letter will be answered, but all will be forwarded. Please write to:

Donald Tyson
C/o Llewellyn Worldwide
P.O. Box 64383, Dept. K749-8
St. Paul, MN 55164-0383 U.S.A.

Please enclose a self-addressed, stamped envelope for reply or $1.00 to cover costs. If outside the U.S.A., please enclose an international postal reply coupon.

DONALD TYSON

READING FORTUNES

MAKING CHARMS

RUNE DICE DIVINATION

DOING MAGIC

1997
Llewellyn Publications
St. Paul, MN 55164-0383
U.S.A.

Cover design: Tom Grewe
Editing and book design: Amy Rost

FIRST EDITION
First Printing, 1997

Library of Congress Cataloging In-Publication Data
Tyson, Donald, 1954–
    Rune dice divination: reading fortunes, doing magic & making charms / Donald Tyson. — 1st ed.
        p. cm.
    Includes bibliographical references.
    ISBN 1-56718-749-8 (trade paper)
    ISBN 1-56718-748-X (kit)
        1. Fortune-telling by runes. 2. Divination.        I. Title.
BF1891.R85T87  1997
133.3'3—dc21                                                97-21570
                                                              CIP

**Publisher's Note**

Llewellyn Publications
A Division of Llewellyn Worldwide, Ltd.
P.O. Box 64383
St. Paul, MN 55164-0383, U.S.A.

# Other Books by the Author

*The New Magus*, 1988

*Rune Magic*, 1988

*The Truth About Ritual Magic*, 1989

*The Truth About Runes*, 1989

*How to Make and Use a Magic Mirror*,
Llewellyn, 1990; Phoenix Publishing, 1995

*Ritual Magic*, 1991

*The Messenger* (fiction), 1993

*Tetragrammaton*, 1995

*New Millennium Magic*, 1996

*Scrying for Beginners*, 1997

*The Tortuous Serpent* (fiction), 1997

# Editor and Annotator

*Three Books of Occult Philosophy*,
Written by Cornelius Agrippa of Nettesheim, 1993

# Other Kits and Cards

*Rune Magic* Deck, 1988

*Power of the Runes* Kit, 1989

# Forthcoming

*Enochian Magic for Beginners*

# Contents

# Figures and Tables

## Chapter Ten

## Chapter Eleven

## Chapter Twelve

## Chapter Thirteen

## Chapter Fourteen

## Chapter Fifteen

## Chapter Seventeen

# THE ORIGIN OF RUNE DICE

■——The concept of rune dice came to me in 1984 during the writing of my book *Rune Magic*. While researching the ways runes were used for divination and magic by the shamans of northern Europe, I asked myself what would be the ideal medium for the runes in modern times. Dice immediately suggested themselves. They are small, light, and durable, making them easy to carry in the pocket. The entire German rune alphabet can be placed on just four dice. The rune dice can be cast in an instant anywhere there is an open space, and they can be read at a single glance.

Dice are as old as the runes themselves. They are connected with divination by the fall of lots in ancient Greece and Egypt. The Teutonic tribes that first developed and spread the runes across the north were renowned for their love of gambling with dice. It is even possible that runes were placed on dice for gaming purposes, although no physical evidence or explicit historical mention of this use has survived. This ancient connection between dice and divination by lots made dice especially attractive as a medium for the runes.

In *Rune Magic* I was able to describe the construction of rune dice and give a basic form of divination using the dice, but there was insufficient space in that book to fully explore the possibilities of the dice as both an oracle and an instrument for active ritual magic. For years I longed to return to the dice and give them the attention I was convinced they deserved, but other writing projects always got in the way. When I was asked to write a book devoted to the rune dice, I jumped at the chance. You are holding the result in your hands.

In *Rune Magic* I invented three primary media to carry the runes—rune wands, rune cards, and rune dice. Rune wands represent my attempt to re-create the ancient pagan form of divination by runes that was in use during the time of the Roman Empire. Rune cards were inspired by the Tarot. Although I came up with the concept independently, another deck of rune cards (quite different from mine) appeared around the same time as the *Rune Magic Cards*, so I cannot claim with absolute certainty to be the first person to put the runes on cards. However, I am confident that I was the first to place the runes on dice.

Of the three media, the rune dice are my personal favorite. There is a sheer elegance and sense of rightness about putting the runes onto dice that is not equaled by any other rune system. You will come to appreciate this as you gain familiarity with the dice. By knowing a few basic principles of divination by the fall of lots, it is possible to gain a complex response to virtually any human question with a single cast of the dice. All but one of the methods of divination described in this book are single-cast methods. A technique using multiple casts has been added for the sake of completeness.

Over the years I have studied and used many forms of divination. Based on this experience, I can state unequivocally that rune dice is the clearest, simplest, and most precise system for investigating unknown matters of the past, present, or future. Once you know what the runes mean, and have learned how to interpret the fall of the dice in a cast, you will be able to gain a detailed and exact response to any question in moments. There is a refreshing lack of ambiguity in the runes due to their simple root meanings. This clarity in the meaning will carry over into your readings.

When rune cards are laid down in a spread, the pattern is predetermined. This limits the amount of information that can be extracted from it. The diviner is forced to draw most of the meaning from the runes that appear on the cards themselves. On the other hand, when rune wands or rune stones are allowed to fall randomly, the usefulness of the pattern they form is overwhelmed by the sheer number of runes that must be considered. Too much information can be just as great a hindrance in divination as too little information.

Rune dice strike a perfect balance between the complexity and subtlety of interpretation that arises from the unique pattern created by the cast, and the inherent simplicity that results when the divination is limited to four runes. Because there are only four dice, the pattern never becomes too complicated to read. Yet every cast generates a pattern that has never before existed. It comes into being solely in conjunction with the question for which the runes were cast. An enormous amount of useful information can be extracted from the way the dice fall in relation to one another.

An additional level of meaning has been introduced into single-cast divination through pattern matrices. A pattern matrix is a grid that divides the surface upon which the dice are cast into significant zones.

This allows rune divination with single casts of the dice to be tailored to specific areas of investigation, such as whole-life readings, questions that relate to time, family readings, relationships, and so on.

It is not necessary to use these matrices when divining with rune dice, but they can be helpful. All the matrices are simple enough that anyone can draw them on a sheet of newspaper or scratch them on the ground in a few seconds. You do not need to buy anything or spend a lot of time making anything to use the pattern matrices.

This book is mainly about divination by rune dice, but it also describes how to use the dice for ritual magic. Magic was the primary function of the runes in Roman times, and divination was just one form of this magic (though probably the most important). It is harder to understand how to use the runes for ritual work than to create techniques of rune divination. For this reason most modern writers neglect rune magic in favor of divination. I have attempted to restore the balance, at least partially, by resurrecting the ancient process of rune magic used by the shamans of the north. The steps of this ritual process are applied to the construction of rune charms. Rune dice are used in the making of these charms.

One of the most important aspects of this book, which will not be found elsewhere, is the emphasis laid upon the rune gods. If they are to be effective, the runes must be recognized as sigils or emblems of spiritual beings who embody and control specific forces of the natural and supernatural worlds. To conceive the runes as the emblems of living gods is to understand them as the ancient rune masters understood them. It allows the fundamental energies of the runes to be accessed. It is not possible to awaken the powers of the runes if they are regarded merely as letters for writing.

This book was written to allow you to utilize the full potential of rune dice, as I have been using them in my own work for the last decade. They are my favorite instrument of divination. I hope they will become your favorite also. The longer I use them, the more clearly I perceive their inherent beauty, which stems from a perfect marriage of form and function. I am proud to have ushered rune dice into the world, and if this is your first experience with them, I am equally proud to introduce them to you.

# THE BIRTH OF RUNES

## ■ The Legacy of Woden

Legend says that the runes were born in the fiery womb of the Earth, at the roots of the great ash tree, Yggdrasill, that is the axle of the ever-turning universe. The three roots of the world ash reach down to the very center of creation. Its lofty boughs separate sky from ground and maintain the order of the cosmos. Were Yggdrasill to die, the sky would crash to the Earth, the two would become mixed together and chaos would obliterate time.

It was Woden (Odin to the Norse) who first found the runes and brought them forth from their hiding place. Woden is the Teutonic god of magic and also the father of the human race. The All-Father captured the runes after a torturous trial of his courage and his will to endure. For nine days and nights he hung suspended from Yggdrasill, gashed on his body by a blade so that his blood ran freely, taking neither food nor drink.

At the end of his ordeal he experienced a vision. The ground seemed to open under him, and he saw down to the very root of creation itself. There resided the runes, glowing with balefire. Eagerly Woden snatched them up, but the strain was too great for him to endure. With a roaring scream he passed into unconsciousness. When he awoke the runes remained with him. They are his precious legacy to his mortal children.

Boasting of his great achievement in the edda called the *Havamal*, Woden himself declares:

> *Well-being I won*
> *and wisdom too,*
> *I grew and joyed in my growth—*
> *from a word to a word*
> *I was led to a word,*
> *From a deed to another deed.*

## Initiation Rite of the Shamans

The story of Woden's winning of the runes is only a myth, but myths exist to preserve and convey truths to future generations of humanity. The religion of the ancient Teutonic tribes of northern Europe was shamanism. Their gods and goddesses, spirits and demons, resided in the forces of the natural world and animated natural places and things. The ordeal of Woden described in the *Havamal* is probably very similar to the trial of initiation undergone by young men seeking to become shamans. A shaman considered himself the living incarnation of Woden, the god of magic.

The initiate probably cut himself with a blade in diagonal slashes across his chest, and perhaps his arms and legs as well, then allowed himself to be tied naked to a post or a living tree that represented Yggdrasill. He may have used the blade of a spear—the spear is the weapon of Woden. From a line in the *Prose Edda* of Snorri Sturluson we learn that Yggdrasill was sprinkled with white clay, so the pillar or tree to which the initiate was bound was very likely covered with white pigment. The body of the initiate may also have been painted white. White is the color of death, and thus rebirth.

The initiate was left tied to the representation of the sacred tree for nine days and nights. We do not know how he was tied, but the *Havamal* says that Woden hung from the tree and swung there for nine nights, so young shamans may have been suspended in some way. Probably the rite was accompanied by the chanting, singing, drumming, and dancing of other members of the tribe. At the end of the ordeal, if the initiate still remained alive, he was given the secret wisdom of the runes by his teacher, who was probably his father since shamanism was considered to be a hereditary talent. In this way old Woden passed on the sacred knowledge of runes to young Woden, who sacrificed himself (as Woden incarnate) to himself (as Woden the god) on the tree as payment for this precious legacy, and so renewed himself through the hereditary line of shamans.

## The Spread of Rune Wisdom

If this reconstruction of the initiatory rite of Teutonic shamans is correct, then runes were the central wisdom teaching of the cult of Woden. Runes embodied the magic power of the shaman. His possession of runes proved his direct line of descent from the All-Father. The shaman would have guarded this precious wisdom with his life. Yet over centuries, bits and pieces of rune lore became known to men and women who had not undergone the formal nine-day rite of initiation.

In historic times it was common for women to possess at least a portion of the rune lore. Such women lived apart, and were consulted by the tribe for divination, healing, and the casting of spells. They were the forerunners of the rural wise women of Europe, who where so cruelly persecuted by the Christian Church as witches. Common warriors, the young men who swore allegiance to a chief and fought for him in return for their food, shelter, and possessions, also gained a smattering of rune wisdom. They used the runes to give themselves extra courage in battle, protect themselves from weapons and fire, calm storms at sea, and other matters that pertained to their occupation.

Eventually, village scribes came to use the runes in more common ways to keep track of the passage of days and to record important events and business transactions. Some of these rune calendars and records have survived, but they appear to have little if any magical significance. During the Middle Ages monks kept some of the rune lore alive by recording the runes in their manuscripts. This was seen as an amusement and a test of the reader's depth of learning. A monk who could not read the runes was looked upon as poorly educated. It is also very likely that runes were used for gaming purposes, although no explicit record of gambling with runes has survived. Frequently systems of divination devolve into games of chance.

## The Historic Birth of Runes

The shamans who had long forgotten the true origin of the runes explained the runes' existence with the myth that Woden snatched the runes out of the ground. How runes really began is not known for certain. It is thought that they were created by a shaman, or group of shamans, traveling with Germanic mercenaries in northern Italy around 500 B.C. There are definite traces of the Etruscan and Latin alphabets in the runes.

Shamans used simple symbols for magic long before the invention of runes. These basic symbols of magic, which are preserved in rock carvings, were merged with the letters of the Etruscan alphabet to create characters that were used by the shamans both to record important information, and to embody magic forces. At a later date elements from the Latin alphabet were added.

It is important to understand that runes are symbols similar to the letters of the alphabet. They are not the objects or materials upon which they are inscribed. There is really no such thing as a "rune stone," merely a stone upon which a rune has been written. Runes can lend their power to an object upon which they are marked, but the object and the runes upon it are two separate things.

Over time, roving German mercenaries carried runes throughout Europe. The Vikings took them even farther afield on their voyages of pillage and discovery. More than forty rune carvings have supposedly been found in the New World. Two of the most famous (or infamous) rune stones were purported to have been discovered in Nova Scotia and Minnesota.

All examples of runes in North America have been dismissed as fakes by experts. However, we know that the Vikings settled in Newfoundland and explored other parts of North America; we also know that the Vikings used runes, so it is almost certain that runes were used for magical purposes in North America. If legitimate rune relics are ever discovered in the New World, it will probably be in Newfoundland, Nova Scotia, or on the coast of Labrador, where Viking activity was concentrated.

# The Rune Alphabets

As tribal societies more and more distant from each other used the runes over a span of centuries, the runes evolved into three general forms. The oldest and purest, from a magical point of view, is the original Germanic twenty-four-rune alphabet, known as the *futhark* from its first six characters (*F, U, Th, A, R, K*). This was used in earliest times in the region of the Alps and in what is now Germany. It is the runes of the futhark that appear on the rune dice. These runes have the most extensive history as instruments of magic.

The second form of the rune alphabet developed in Scandinavia. At first it was the original German runes that were used by the forefathers of the Viking rovers, but over time the twenty-four runes of the futhark were reduced to sixteen to suit the Scandinavian languages. No new runes were invented—eight were simply dropped. This process of change was completed in Denmark around the ninth century and quickly spread into Sweden and Norway. The result was two closely related futharks of sixteen runes, the Danish and the Swedish-Norwegian. The Vikings carried their reduced set of runes to Iceland when they settled that bleak, volcanic island.

Some of the Scandinavian runes have modified shapes that distinguish them from the corresponding Germanic originals, but it is usually possible to see the similarity in shape between related runes. We will not concern ourselves with the Scandinavian runes. Because of their reduced number and late development they have a limited usefulness in magic and divination.

The third transformation of the runes began in Friesland (the Netherlands) among the Anglo-Saxon tribes, but did not reach its final form until carried by the Anglo-Saxons into England. Exactly the opposite change occurred from that which took place in Scandinavia. Instead of discarding some runes and adding multiple sound values to those that remained to suit their language requirements, the Anglo-Saxons kept all the original runes and added entirely new runes. Two English *futhorcs* developed, the older one having twenty-eight runes and the later version having thirty-three runes. The new runes were simply added to the end of the original twenty-four Germanic runes.

The Anglo-Saxons made some changes in the forms of some runes, but not such extensive changes as the Norse. They also inverted the positions of the final two runes in the German futhark before adding their new runes to the end. These changes began in Friesland in the fifth century, but were only completed in Northumbria in the ninth century. It was a gradual evolution over many generations, not the decision of any one shaman or chief. Since some of the runes have different sounds when pronounced in Old English, the English rune alphabet is called the futhorc (*F, U, Th, O, R, C*) even though the first six runes are the same runes as those of the Germanic futhark.

In this book I have given both the Germanic and Old English names for the runes. The Old English names are the names by which these same runes were called in England. They appear in parentheses after the German names. It is useful to know the Old English names because the runes are often referred to by these names in books about magic and divination. It must be understood, however, that the rune dice are inscribed with the twenty-four German runes (some of the same English runes have slightly different forms). The German futhark is the oldest, the purest, and the most powerful of the rune alphabets.

# Rune Families

The futhark has two main divisions. One of these divisions is acknowledged by scholars to have existed from the earliest descriptions of the runes. It may be as old as the runes themselves. This is the division of the futhark into three families, called *aettir* by the Norse. Each *aett* contains eight runes, and is named after the rune that begins it. The three aettir are Fehu (Feoh), Hagalaz (Haegl), and Teiwaz (Tir). Each of these runes is the leader or father of its family.

We do not know for certain what this division of the runes was used for in ancient times, but it must have been very important. Even when the runes were reduced to sixteen in Scandinavia, the Norse still divided them into three groups of six, five, and five, and still called these groups by their old names. Similarly, even after the runes were increased to twenty-eight (and later thirty-three) in England, the old division into families was not forgotten.

# Rune Pairs

The second important division of the runes, which is not recognized by scholars because it does not appear explicitly recorded on the ancient relics or in manuscripts, is the division of the runes into pairs. When we divide the runes of the futhark into twelve groups of two, we find that a strong relationship exists between the runes in each pair. Sometimes this relationship is contrasting; sometimes it is complementary.

In my opinion the existence of rune pairs is undeniable. It has great utility when using the runes for divination. The meaning of any rune can only be completely understood by considering it in connection with the other rune of its pair.

For example, the first rune is Fehu (Feoh), which means *cattle*, a domesticated beast used by the ancient Germans as a measure of wealth. The second rune is Uruz (Ur), which means *aurochs*, a fierce wild ox that was hunted by young German men as a test of their manhood. Thus, Fehu signifies mildness, subservience, and possession, whereas Uruz signifies ferocity, rebellion, and freedom. The first is the tamed and the second the untamable. The first is the possessed and the second the unpossessable. The first is the conquered and the second the unconquerable.

## The Original Shapes of the Runes

The runes on the dice show the forms of the Germanic futhark, with the exception of several runes that appear with curved or horizontal lines in surviving examples of the futhark. Although runes were cut into a large variety of materials for magic, they were most often carved on small wands or staffs. There is general agreement that in the beginning all the runes had only vertical and diagonal strokes so that they would be easier to cut into the wands with a knife across the grain of the wood. A curved line is very difficult to carve into wood; a horizontal line might be concealed by a crack in the wand, or the wand might be split while carving it.

The way an ancient shaman probably cut runes was to roll the blade of his knife part of the way around the side of a slender twig or wand in order to cut off a thin wedge of tender new bark. This revealed the white wood beneath. With a little practice this technique became second nature. It also caused the freshly cut wand to "bleed" sap, the life force of the tree. The sap was probably considered to nourish the runes. (In the case of alder twigs, which turn bright red when the naked wood is exposed to the open air, this transformation must have been quite striking.)

Over the centuries runes began to be cut into stone and scratched into metal and bone surfaces, such as the blades of swords, the rims of shields, the bands of amulet rings, and the backs of combs. On these surfaces it was not necessary to always use vertical or diagonal strokes when making the runes, and the original shapes began to be corrupted with curved and horizontal lines. Although most of the futhark runes retain their original shapes, some (Uruz, Wunjo, Jera) are often shown with curves, and one (Inguz) is shown with horizontal lines.

I have restored the runes to their original shapes on the rune dice. There is general agreement among rune scholars that these are the earliest shapes of the Germanic runes. The rune masters of the Teutonic tribes would have used these forms of the runes to work their magic at the time of Julius Caesar, who was the first Roman writer to explicitly mention the runes.

## The Use of Runes in Magic

As the centuries passed, runes were used more and more for mundane purposes, such as recording information and keeping calendars. The magical function of runes continued along with their writing function, and undoubtedly runes were still being used for magic and divination right up until they were officially outlawed in Iceland in 1639. However, because examples of the use of runes for writing on stone monuments have survived (whereas examples of their magical use for the most part have not survived) many scholars are under the mistaken notion that the magical use of runes was mainly restricted to the early centuries of their development. In my opinion, this is not so. Magic was then, as it is now, an esoteric art. Writing, by its nature, is exoteric. Writing must be seen to be of any value, and magic frequently must not be seen if it is to work as intended.

I believe that the primary use for runes was always magical, at least until the sixteenth century or so when the magical use of runes may have begun to suffer neglect due to the increasing dominance of Christianity in the lives of the rural folk of the northlands. Since their beginning, the most important magical use for runes has always been divination. The modern rune revival has in large measure occurred because of the ease with which runes may be used to reveal hidden or future matters. It is to this central function of the runes that the present book is mainly devoted.

## The Gods of the Runes

Some of the names of the runes are recognized as the names of Teutonic gods and demons. Teiwaz (Tir) is a version of the name Tyr or Tew, the ancient god who gives Tuesday its name. Tew was associated by the Romans with their god Mars. Inguz (Ing) was the fertility god of the Ingwine, or Danes—*ing* is another word for meadow, a place of fertile soil. Ansuz (Os) literally means god, and was interpreted in the *Icelandic Rune Poem* as another term for Woden. Thurisaz (Thorn), by contrast, means giant or demon. Probably a specific demon was intended.

The names of the other runes are not known to have been derived from the names of gods and goddesses, but there is reason to believe this may have been the case. The gods of the Teutonic tribes were originally personifications of the forces of nature. Most of the runes represent natural forces. The shamanic religion of the north deified certain species of animals and employed them as totems. Some of the runes are named for these totemic beasts. The rune Mannaz (Man) refers to human beings, but the reference is specifically to the first man, the divine hero of the human race. Several runes refer to human qualities or experiences such as Wunjo (glory) and Nauthaz (endurance), but even in these cases there is good reason to suspect that these inner forces were in early times regarded as gods, even as Fate and Fortune and Wisdom were treated as goddesses by the Romans.

In my opinion, all of the original runes of the futhark are deities worshiped by the Teutonic tribes in prehistoric times. When the runes came to be immortalized in the Norse sagas and recorded in manuscripts by Christian monks, most of these gods and goddesses had long since been forgotten. Only a few of the most important were still recognized.

In magic, the runes themselves were treated as potent, self-aware entities with the power to grant gifts or exact payments. Each rune symbol is the living embodiment of a god or spirit. The symbol of the rune should be regarded as the sigil of the god, and the name of the rune as the name of the god. This is not so unusual a concept as might first appear. In the esoteric philosophy of the Jewish Kabbalah, each letter is looked upon as an independent power that has sprung from the utterance of God. The letters are treated almost as angels. In the system of magic delivered by the Enochian spirits to the Elizabethan mathematician Dr. John Dee, individual Enochian letters are both the names of angels and the angels themselves.

When we conceive the rune symbols as living gods, we achieve a more accurate and immediate appreciation of their importance. They were regarded in this way by the shamans of ancient times, who risked death during the ceremony of initiation to learn their meanings. To know the names and characteristics of the rune gods was to gain a measure of control over them.

The initiated shaman became an awakened child of Woden, and gloried in his spiritual gifts. Using the basic magical tools of the runes he was able to construct many potent amulets and spells, and to pierce the distance of time and space. He controlled the flow of information between the gods of the runes and the people of his tribe. In this capacity of gatekeeper of the gods he was both revered and feared by the common people.

Runes have not lost their ancient power. The rune gods still live. In secret places modern shamans continue to call upon them in their old, forgotten names. And the gods continue to respond, granting gifts in exchange for self-sacrifice and dedication.

CHAPTER TWO

# HOW DIVINATION WORKS

■───── ## "What Is Below Is Like That Which Is Above"

Woden was fabled to have snatched up the runes from their resting place at the roots of the world ash, Yggdrasill. In the creation myth of the north, the first man was made from an ash tree. The esoteric meaning of this double appearance of the ash is that a human being is a smaller version of the universe, but identical to it in all its essential aspects. Man is the microcosm (little world) and the universe is the macrocosm (big world). This underlying unity of human nature and world nature is expressed in the famous line from the ancient document known as the Smaragdine (Emerald Tablet) of Hermes Trismegistus:

> What is below is like that which is above, and what is above is like that which is below, to accomplish the miracle of the One Thing.

A human being is inextricably joined to the universe by mind. What we think of as ourselves—our thoughts and dreams, our desires and fears, our memories and intuitions—exists only in mind. Similarly, what we think of as the larger universe—the ground and sky, the mountains and oceans, the stars and galaxies—also exists only in mind. Mind is all that we can perceive or conceive. Everything that has being is the expression of a single, undivided consciousness.

That is what Hermes means when he says "what is above is like that which is below." Since both macrocosm and microcosm, cosmic nature and human nature, are created by mind within mind, they must be intimately related to each other.

## The Nature of Self

This is a hard concept to come to terms with, but it is important, because all types of divination depend on this essential unity of the little world of the human being and the greater world of land and sea and stars. At first we tend to reject the idea that the universe lies within our mind. The difference between what is "out there" in the wide world and what is "in here" in what we call the self seems so obvious. However, when we think about it more carefully we realize that it is not so easy to draw the line between what is inside and what is outside.

Is our body inside or outside? Does it belong to what we conceive as self or to the world at large? If we lose a leg, are we really losing some of our essential identity as a human being, or are we still a whole person? What about our name? When we change our name do we change the self? Are memories a part of our essential being? If so, what happens when we forget?

Some individuals look upon their children or their lover as a part of themselves. In primitive cultures it is common for members of a tribe to view themselves as organs of a greater human body. When they are exiled from the tribe for violating the law they cannot function because they feel cut off from a necessary and vital part of their own nature. Like roses snipped away from their stems, they sicken and eventually die. The extended family or clan is viewed in much the same way. In societies that use totemic animals, the totem of a clan is seen as a part of the clan, and thus a part of the self of every member of the clan.

The primitive view extends the self beyond the boundary of the body, but usually stops far short of embracing all of creation. The modern scientific view limits the self to the body, or increasingly to the tissues of the brain, but stops short of rejecting all physical matter.

Both the primitive view of self and the modern scientific view are wrong. Identity is both everything in the universe, because everything exists within mind, and nothing in the universe, because mind is not a physical object. It is just as absurd to say that your essential identity is contained within your brain as it is to say that your identity is contained in a chair across the room. Yet brain and chair are created by mind from mind within mind, and mind is indeed self.

## A Magical View of Reality

To understand the underlying unity of microcosm and macrocosm is to achieve a magical view of reality. It explains why small events, such as the fall of a set of rune dice, can resonate with and reveal aspects of much larger and more distant events, such as a future marriage or the birth of a child. Because all is mind, these two happenings must in some way be connected. It is the task of the diviner to perceive and interpret the macrocosmic event by the microcosmic event he or she has deliberately generated. Sometimes the diviner takes the opposite approach and interprets smaller events in the lives of human beings by larger events in nature, such as the appearance of a comet or a long drought. This is divination by omens or portents, and was usually applied to important persons such as kings or military leaders.

The link between microcosm and macrocosm was used in ancient times to justify the grandmother of all divination, astrology. It provided a reason distant stars and planets, so impersonal and remote, influenced details in the lives of individual human beings. More perceptive scholars such as Saint Augustine and Thomas Aquinas did not dismiss the effectiveness of astrology, but they drew the important distinction between a human life being directed by the stars and a human life reflected in the pattern of the stars. They believed that the movements of the heavenly spheres did not determine the affairs of human beings (or what good was human free will?), but rather that the unity between man and the heavens caused the events in every human life to be mirrored and revealed in the movements of the heavens to those who had the wisdom to read these motions.

The rays of astrology, which are straight lines drawn between places on the surface of the Earth and the stars and planets at a given time, and the aspects of astrology, which are the angles formed by these rays (the Earth is always conceived to lie at the center of the zodiac), do not conduct some mysterious occult energy from the heavens down to the Earth. Their arrangement merely expresses the connection between events on the Earth and events in the heavens at a given moment in time.

# Synchronicity

The psychologist Carl Jung coined a new word to describe this relationship between little things and big things. He called it *synchronicity*, the meaningful connection in time between physically unconnected events. Another more common word for the same thing is *coincidence*. Coincidences are usually dismissed as unimportant. Synchronicities are by definition significant and meaningful connected happenings. Usually synchronistic events happen at the same moment, or the span of time between the first and later events is perceived to be significant.

For example, if a woman has a dream that the plane she is on will crash at 4:15 P.M., and the next afternoon at 4:15 the plane she intended to fly on actually does crash, this is synchronicity. If a man feels a stabbing pain in his left wrist, and later discovers that his twin brother has had an accident in which his left hand was cut off at the same time, it is a synchronicity. Events very similar to these examples have actually occurred. Synchronicity depends on the unity of microcosm and macrocosm in mind.

The diviner seeks to attain synchronicity in a deliberate way using mechanical means. A Tarot reader attempts to discern the underlying connection between the pattern of the cards in a spread and the future life of the person who has come in to have his or her fortune read. Because of the underlying link between all things, the Tarot reader believes that the position of the cards can be influenced and made to reflect the life of the querent by concentrating on the cards and on the question being asked at the same time.

Rune dice work the same way. The dice and the person seeking to learn the future are both a part of mind. By concentrating on the question of the reading and on the dice at the same time, the two are related in the mind of the reader in a heightened and significant manner. It is then easier to discern the connection between the relationship and relative positions of the runes on the dice and the events surrounding the question.

It is not that the rune diviner changes the fall of the rune dice by thinking about them. When the diviner concentrates on the dice with the question of the reading strongly in mind, a synchronistic link is created between the meaning already inherent in the pattern of the dice and the hidden or future events in the life of the querent. To the diviner, it appears as if the pattern of the dice has been changed to increase its meaning, because the diviner is able to gather such a wealth of clear, precise information from the pattern.

Synchronicities are occurring every moment of every day in the life of every human being. There is a connection between the smallest happening in your life and the greatest world event, but you do not recognize the connection. If you did recognize these innumerable links you would be hailed as a great prophet. Divination seeks to make some of those connections into meaningful synchronous events. The mechanism of divination, whether it is an astrological chart, a deck of Tarot cards, tea leaves in the bottom of a cup, or a set of rune dice, merely focuses the mind in a very specific and precise way so that the existing linkages can be perceived and correctly interpreted.

## Divination Is an Intuitive Act

It is not really necessary to have a theory about the way divination works to successfully perform a divination. Reading the runes is an intuitive act, and it requires an innate personal gift. The best diviners are usually not the most intelligent or highly educated members of society. They are those who can perceive the underlying connection between little things and big things. We call this power *intuition*.

Diviners need to be intuitive if the runes are ever to speak to them and reveal their secrets. It is not enough merely to know the written meanings of the runes and the significance of the patterns they make when they are cast. A good diviner is always open to receive subtle currents of perception. Whether these currents flow from the runes, the person seeking the reading, the stars, or the rune gods is less important than correctly interpreting their meaning in relation to the question.

It is usually easier to do an accurate reading for someone else than for yourself. Many diviners will not do self-readings. When we try to predict events in our own life, our emotions and needs and fears get in the way of our intuition and destroy our judgment. It may be likened to a doctor who tries to operate on himself, or a lawyer who represents herself in court. Most of us are experts at self-deception. This is fine in our daily lives, but when we do a divination we must always be completely impartial and honest.

## Respect the Runes

The danger that comes from disrespecting the runes is greater than simply an inaccurate reading. Once the runes are treated in a dishonest way, and the diviner tries to influence their meaning in his or her own favor, they cease to give an accurate reading even when the reading is made for somebody else. They become polluted by the insincerity and bias of the diviner. It is a long time before this psychic dirt wears off. The same thing happens when the runes are treated as toys to be played with, or regarded with indifference. Even if the diviner later realizes the power and majesty of the runes, it may be months or years before they begin to read true once again, if ever.

You will not fall into this fatal error if you always look upon each rune as a living god. The name of the rune is the name of the god, the shape of the rune is the sigil of the god, the power of the rune is the life-force of the god, and the function of the rune is the office of the god. With this in mind, you will come to the runes with a respectful attitude and handle them with care. You will always keep the dice clean, and always store them in a safe place that is in harmony with their nature and purpose. You will never show them to others unless you are doing a reading on their behalf, and above all will never allow anyone else to touch or handle the dice unless they are casting them so that you can perform their reading.

A simple rule applies. If you treat the runes as though they are powerful, they will be powerful. If you treat them as though they have the ability to reveal secrets, they will reveal secrets. If you treat them as though they can show the future, they will indeed show the future to you. On the other hand, if you treat the runes as playthings for your amusement, they will never be of any importance. If you doubt that they will work, they will never work. If you treat the runes with scorn or contempt, the rune gods will in turn treat you with scorn and contempt. They may even cause you to fall sick or become injured.

It is best to adopt a completely professional manner every time you pick up the dice to perform a reading. Do not joke with others or behave in a frivolous way. Take care not to use bad language. Always wash your hands and cleanse your breath before handling the dice. Maintain a calm mind and a gentle, positive emotional state. Never use the runes when you are angry, or depressed, or worried. Never use the runes when you are tired or sick.

Following these precepts is far more important, in the long run, than memorizing all the meanings of the runes, and even more important than inherent psychic ability. No matter how much you know about the runes, or how psychic you may be, if you treat the runes with disrespect they will refuse to work for you. Once they have turned their backs on you, it will be a long time before you can induce them to favor your purposes again. It is a lot harder to win back the rune gods than it is to treat them properly in the first place.

# MEANINGS OF THE RUNES

## ■——Root Meanings of the Runes

In Table 3.1 on the following pages, I have shown the forms and given the names for the runes in all three of the major branches that occurred in their history. However, because this book is concerned mainly with the twenty-four Germanic runes that appear on the rune dice, the additional runes in the two forms of the Old English futhorc have not been examined. You will find detailed explanations of the meanings of these additional runes in my book *Rune Magic*.

Each rune may be interpreted in relation to the life of the querent on a physical, emotional, intellectual, or spiritual level. The level of meaning that applies in any given circumstance is determined by the context of the cast in which the rune falls and the nature of the question. Often more than one interpretation is possible at the same time. All meanings of the runes, from the tangible to the abstract, stem from the root meanings embodied in their names.

## Germanic

| Aett | Runes | Names |
|------|-------|-------|
| First | ᚠ | Fehu |
| | ᚢ | Uruz |
| | ᚦ | Thurisaz |
| | ᚨ | Ansuz |
| | ᚱ | Raido |
| | ᚲ | Kano |
| | ᚷ | Gebo |
| | ᚹ | Wunjo |
| Second | ᚺ | Hagalaz |
| | ᚾ | Nauthiz |
| | ᛁ | Isa |
| | ᛃ | Jera |
| | ᛇ | Eihwaz |
| | ᛈ | Perth |
| | ᛉ | Algiz |
| | ᛊ | Sowelu |

## Old English

| Aett | Runes | Names |
|------|-------|-------|
| First | ᚠ | Feoh |
| | ᚢ | Ur |
| | ᚦ | Thorn |
| | ᚩ | Os |
| | ᚱ | Rad |
| | ᚳ | Cen |
| | ᚷ | Gyfu |
| | ᚹ | Wyn |
| Second | ᚻ | Haegl |
| | ᚾ | Nyd |
| | ᛁ | Is |
| | ᛄ | Ger |
| | ᛇ | Eoh |
| | ᛈ | Peordh |
| | ᛉ | Eolh |
| | ᛋ | Sigel |

## Old Norse

| Aett | Runes | Names |
|------|-------|-------|
| First | ᚠ | Fehu |
| | ᚢ | UruR |
| | ᚦ | ThurisaR |
| | ᚬ | AsuR |
| | ᚱ | Raidhu |
| | ᚴ | Kauna |
| Second | ᚼ | Hagla |
| | ᚾ | NaudhiR |
| | ᛁ | IsaR |
| | ᛅ | Jara |
| | ᛋ | Sowelu |

## Third

|  |  |
|---|---|
| ↑ | Teiwaz |
| ᛒ | Berkana |
| Μ | Ehwaz |
| Χ | Mannaz |
| ᛚ | Laguz |
| ◇ | Inguz |
| Μ | Dagaz |
| Χ | Othila |

## Third

|  |  |
|---|---|
| ↑ | Tir |
| ᛒ | Beorc |
| Μ | Eh |
| Χ | Man |
| ᛚ | Lagu |
| ᛜ | Ing |
| Χ | Ethel |
| Η | Daeg |

## Additional Runes

|  |  |
|---|---|
| ᚪ | Ac |
| ᚫ | Aesc |
| ᛇ | Yr |
| ↑ | Ear |
| ᚼ | Ior |
| ᚳ | Calc |
| ᚷ | Gar |
| ᛁ | Cweordh |
| Μ | Stan |

## Third

|  |  |
|---|---|
| ⌐ | TiwaR |
| ᛒ | Berkana |
| Ψ | MannaR |
| ᛚ | LaguR |
| ᛉ | AlgiR |

**TABLE 3.1.** The three historical rune systems.

The root meanings of the runes are usually concrete and basic. For example, Kano (Cen) means a torch, Laguz (Lagu) means water, Isa (Is) means ice, and so on. From these simple material things, it is possible to extrapolate more abstract meanings. For example, fire is symbolically a guide in darkness and a giver of light. Water is associated with dreams, madness, and illusion. Ice is treacherous to walk across, and so may be interpreted to signify danger and betrayal on a symbolic level. Many of these symbolic interpretations of the runes appear in the surviving rune poems, which describe the meanings of the runes with poetic imagery.

Although it has become popular with some New Age writers to find meaning in the shapes of the runes, I have generally avoided this practice because many of the rune forms have no reasonable connection with the meanings of those runes. In a few cases the shapes of the runes do seem to have a direct correspondence with their meanings. These significant forms I have noticed briefly.

Favorable and unfavorable interpretations are determined by the position of the runes in the context of the overall pattern of the cast, and by where the runes fall upon the pattern matrix (the underlying grid) used for the divination. This will be examined in detail under each specific type of divination.

## Inverted and Supine Runes

Some of the runes have a vertically asymmetrical shape that allows them to be read as either upright or inverted. Others do not. In divination, inversion of a symbol generally signifies malice or obstruction. However, where a violent or hurtful rune is involved, inversion can actually lessen its evil effect. Inversion mitigates or modifies the essential upright meaning.

For example, Thurisaz (Thorn) is generally considered an evil rune, but when it appears inverted this evil effect is lessened or turned aside.

The rune diviner can either choose to incorporate the inverted meanings of the asymmetrical runes into the reading, or ignore the orientation of these runes. Inversion plays an important part in Tarot divination, but is not considered so important when reading the runes. Because it is impossible to tell whether a symmetrical rune is upright or inverted on the rune dice, I prefer not to notice the inversion of asymmetrical runes in my divinations with the dice.

Another level of interpretation may be derived from runes that fall horizontal, or supine, from the perspective of the diviner. By supine, I mean that the head of a rune would point either toward nine or three if cast upon the dial of a clock. When a rune falls supine, it stands for inertia, hesitation, or delay in the action signified by this rune in the context of the cast as a whole. When a rune appears to lie supine on its face, from the perspective of the diviner (head at three o'clock), it signifies delay at the end of action; when it lies supine on its back (head at nine o'clock), it signifies delay at the beginning of an action.

Here is a useful little trick to remember the distinction in meaning between inverted and supine runes. Think of inverted runes as standing on their heads, and doing everything topsy-turvy from the way they would commonly act. Inverted runes are crazy. Think of supine runes as lying down on the job, and being slow and reluctant to fulfill their appointed functions. Supine runes are lazy. Runes on their backs are asleep and soon to wake and rise up. Runes on their faces have just fallen asleep and will continue to doze for a long time.

I prefer not to interpret supine runes in a cast, as a general rule, because the runes on the dice seldom fall perfectly aligned. Usually they fall in a diagonal position, and it can be difficult to know whether to interpret them as upright or supine (or inverted or supine). However, I wanted to mention this technique of interpretation because sometimes when it is very difficult to read the runes, their orientation can add a vital level of meaning that makes the whole cast comprehensible. You may use it if you wish, or ignore it as I usually do.

## A Matter of Interpretation

If you are familiar with runes from other books, you may notice that some of my meanings differ from some of the meanings found elsewhere. This is not an error, but a matter of interpretation. We have a good idea from the ancient rune poems and mentions in the eddas what most of the runes mean, but a few are very unclear. For example, no one really knows what the rune Perth (Peordh) means, or what it was used for. References to Perth in the rune poems are ambiguous. I believe it means apple, and signifies the mythic associations of the apple and apple wood, which was employed to mark runes upon, and to make lots for gambling purposes, but this is merely my best judgment based on years of thought and research.

Similarly, we know that the rune Eihwaz (Eoh) means yew, but it is not clear which associations of the yew tree dominated in this rune. Is the rune Eihwaz primarily defined by the association of yew wood with the weapon of warfare, the bow, or by the associations of the yew with graveyards and magic yew wands? Both are important. In this book I have favored the latter association, but you should understand that it is an opinion, not a certainty.

The best course for you to follow is to study the essential meanings of the runes, which for the most part are established and accepted, then try to reason out the symbolic and mythical associations that may be extrapolated from those simple, physical meanings. You will be able to trace the link between the abstract qualities of a rune and its basic meaning if you think about it long enough. In my book *Rune Magic* I have tried to give the entire scope of known and conjectured associations for all the existing runes that have been postulated by modern rune scholars, along with pertinent verses from the ancient rune poems. If you are seeking a deeper understanding of the runes you may wish to read it.

In the interpretations that follow I have given both the German and Old English names of the runes, along with their transliterations, German phonetic values, and Old English phonetic values. The transliterations merely indicate letters of the Latin alphabet that can conveniently be substituted for the runes when using the runes to write messages in English or other modern languages. The transliteration value does not always correspond exactly to the phonetic values.

Some of the sounds in German and Old English are not found in the Latin alphabet. However these may be approximately indicated by combinations of Latin letters. For example, the phonetic value of Eihwaz is a sound midway between the sound (in English) of the vowels *e* and *i*. This may be suggested by the combination *ei*. It is convenient to transliterate Eihwaz with the letter *y*, which otherwise would not have a corresponding rune in the German futhark. Similarly, Wunjo may be transliterated as either *w* or *v* when using the runes for writing. Kano may be transliterated by *k*, *c*, or *q*, even though its phonetic value is *k* in the German runes, and *c* in the English runes.

Bear in mind that these phonetic values are not exact, since it is impossible to indicate an exact sound with only a single letter. For example, the German sound value of Uruz, indicated by *u*, is actually the *oo* sound in the English word *book*. The German phonetic value of the rune Ansuz, indicated here by the letter *a*, is actually the *u* sound in the English word *but*. The single letter, or combinations of two letters, are intended only to give an approximate indication of the sounds of the runes in German and Old English.

## 1. Fehu (Feoh): Cattle

Transliteration: *f*
German sound value: *f*
English sound value: *f*

In ancient times, as in primitive cultures of the present day, cattle represented units of value. The wealth of a person was determined by how many cattle, and slaves, he or she owned. (Cattle and slaves were equated.)

|  |  |
|---:|:---|
| Literal: | Domestic cow. |
| Symbolic: | Valuable possession. |
| Anthropomorphic: | A merchant. |
| Physical: | Food |
| Emotional: | Cowardice. |
| Mental: | Reluctance to try. |
| Spiritual: | Broken will. |

**Favorably Placed**—Moveable possessions, money, wealth, a precious object, increase in income, important purchase, payment of debt, luxury, opulence, power through money, generosity.

**Unfavorably Placed**—Slavery, dependence, bondage to material things, greed, miserliness, cowardice, lack of imagination, stupidity, subservience, a victim mentality, manual labor, poverty.

Upright: Favorable.

Inverted: Unfavorable.

Position: First place, Fehu aett.

Key: Possession.

## 2. Uruz (Ur): Aurochs

Transliteration: *u*
German sound value: *u*
English sound value: *u*

The aurochs was a wild beast similar to a great shaggy ox with the irascible disposition of a bear. It was covered in long black hair and had curled, ram-like horns. The young German warriors hunted it as a test of manhood, and took its horns as trophies to turn into drinking vessels. The horns were rimmed with silver.

Literal: Wild ox.

Symbolic: Male virility.

Anthropomorphic: A soldier.

Physical: Strength.

Emotional: Anger.

Mental: Indomitability.

Spiritual: Liberation.

**Favorably Placed**—Strength, courage, boldness, vitality, sexual potency, freedom, enterprise, dominance, leadership, martial skills.

**Unfavorably Placed**—Rashness, violence, brutality, immaturity, lust, lack of control, unpreparedness, callousness, criminal behavior.

Upright: Favorable.

Inverted: Unfavorable.

Position: Second place, Fehu aett.

Key: Action.

## 3. Thurisaz (Thorn): Devil

Transliteration: *th*

German sound value: *th*

English sound value: *th*

Thorn is the personal name of an evil giant described as the "torturer of women." He is especially associated with the suffering of women, which means menstrual bleeding and the problems of childbirth, including pain, extended labor, the death of the baby, and the death of the mother from excessive bleeding. The embodiment of all that is base, cowardly, and wicked. When this rune occurs in a cast, it signifies bad luck.

Literal: An evil devil.

Symbolic: Cruelty.

Anthropomorphic: An enemy.

Physical: Sickness.

Emotional: Malice.

Mental: Plots.

Spiritual: The abyss.

**Favorably Placed**—Nemesis, poetic justice, purging, catharsis, exposure of malice, falling into one's own trap, just deserts, an evil from which good results, attempt to do harm will backfire.

**Unfavorably Placed**—Malice, lies, vindictiveness, cowardly spite, persecution, envy, jealousy, hatred, deceit, torture, wickedness for its own sake.

Upright: Unfavorable.

Inverted: Favorable.

Position: Third place, Fehu aett.

Key: Evil.

## 4. Ansuz (Os): Wise God

F Transliteration: *a*
German sound value: *a*
English sound value: *o*

This is the father of the gods, Woden, whose wisdom flowed from his mouth like a river. When this rune occurs in a cast, it should be regarded as a sign of good fortune.

Literal: A benevolent god.

Symbolic: Good counsel.

Anthropomorphic: An authority figure.

Physical: Attractive voice.

Emotional: Benevolence.

Mental: Sound judgment.

Spiritual: Tranquillity.

**Favorably Placed**—Wisdom, true words, instruction, eloquence, helpful communication, important message, loving actions, harmony, personal insight, benevolence, protection.

**Unfavorably Placed**—Rigidity, control, obsession with order, fussiness, concern for details, pomposity, authoritarianism, a mother hen, inability to delegate authority, verbosity, punctiliousness.

Upright: Favorable.

Inverted: Unfavorable.

Position: Fourth place, Fehu aett.

Key: Goodness.

## 5. Raido (Rad): Journey by Horse

R Transliteration: *r*
German sound value: *r*
English sound value: *r*

A prolonged land journey, which in ancient times was always undertaken on horseback. By extension, a spiritual quest after enlightenment.

Literal: Travel on horseback.

Symbolic: Quest.

Anthropomorphic: A stranger.

Physical: Labor.

Emotional: Yearning.

Mental: Question.

Spiritual: Seeking.

**Favorably Placed**—Relocation, vacation, change of address, business trip, travel, treasure hunt, personal evolution, quest for enlightenment, escape from evil.

**Unfavorably Placed**—Disruption, dislocation, forced removal, flight from responsibility, journey into darkness, aimlessness, wandering, empty ambitions, chasing rainbows, lack of fulfillment, long illness, possible death.

Upright: Favorable.

Inverted: Unfavorable.

Position: Fifth place, Fehu aett.

Key: Journey.

# 6. Kano (Ken): Torch

Transliteration: *k, c, q*
German sound value: *k*
English sound value: *c*

A manmade flame that illuminates the darkness, such as a torch, lantern, or bonfire. By extension the light of the mind that guides human actions. This rune is also sometimes named Kaunaz or Kenaz. Note that it is half the height of most other runes.

Literal: Guiding flame.

Symbolic: Light of spirit.

Anthropomorphic: A messenger.

Physical: Vitality.

Emotional: Hope.

Mental: Concentration.

Spiritual: Inspiration.

**Favorably Placed**—Guidance, direction, revelation, illumination, reason, answer, goal, light in darkness, the mind, realization, solution to a problem.

**Unfavorably Placed**—Exposure, naked truth, realization of futility, loss of hope, shattered dreams, awakening to reality, cold light of day, broken promise, awareness of personal limitations, news of a death, possible suicide attempt.

Upright: Favorable.

Inverted: Unfavorable.

Position: Sixth place, Fehu aett.

Key: Beacon.

## 7. Gebo (Gyfu): Gift

**X**  Transliteration: *g*
German sound value: *g*
English sound value: *g*

A voluntary gift or sacrifice undertaken to attain a greater purpose. This may be a material gift to win the favor of an individual or the sacrifice upon an altar to a higher spiritual power. It is both the gifts of the gods to humans, and the gifts of humans to the gods. A vertically symmetrical rune, it appears the same upright or inverted, and is positive in both attitudes.

Literal: Gift or offering.

Symbolic: Sacrifice of the lower for the higher.

Anthropomorphic: A benefactor.

Physical: A present.

Emotional: Generosity.

Mental: Helpfulness.

Spiritual: Selflessness.

**Favorably Placed**—Inheritance, bequest, donation, presents, raise in pay, unexpected windfall, charitable contribution, endowment, good luck, winnings, a service received or freely given, an offering of assistance.

**Unfavorably Placed**—Duty, obligation, involuntary sacrifice, responsibility, dependents, toll, debt, burdens, required donations or observances, payments, evil consequences of a charitable act.

Upright: Favorable.

Inverted: Favorable.

Position: Seventh place, Fehu aett.

Key: Sacrifice.

# 8. Wunjo (Wyn): Glory

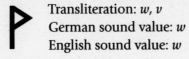

Transliteration: *w, v*
German sound value: *w*
English sound value: *w*

Joy or glory that stems from voluntary offerings. The fruits of sacrifice, which on a spiritual level are ecstasy, and on a temporal level, power.

| | |
|---:|:---|
| Literal: | Glory. |
| Symbolic: | Spiritual exaltation. |
| Anthropomorphic: | A hero. |
| Physical: | Victory. |
| Emotional: | Exuberance. |
| Mental: | Solution or answer. |
| Spiritual: | Ecstasy. |

**Favorably Placed**—Victory, achievement, a prize, honors, dignities, celebrity, recognition of accomplishments, exultation, ecstasy, bliss, a divine reward, transcendence, personal well-being.

**Unfavorably Placed**—Intoxication, delirium, wild enthusiasm, unrealistic plans, delusions of grandeur, excessive hopes or expectations, loss of touch with reality, spirit possession, monomania, dreams of glory.

| | |
|---:|:---|
| Upright: | Favorable. |
| Inverted: | Unfavorable. |
| Position: | Eighth place, Fehu aett. |
| Key: | Happiness. |

# 9. Hagalaz (Haegl): Hail

**H** Transliteration: *h*
German sound value: *h*
English sound value: *h*

The violent, destructive force of nature that beats down crops, kills livestock, and destroys homes. It comes without warning from the sky and strikes at random the just and unjust alike. This rune begins and gives its name to the second of the three aettir. It is symmetrical, and unfavorable both upright and inverted.

Literal: Hailstorm.

Symbolic: Blind force of Nature.

Anthropomorphic: Destructive person.

Physical: Headache.

Emotional: Rage.

Mental: Turmoil.

Spiritual: Confusion.

**Favorably Placed**—Triumph over adversity, strengthening through hardship, trial weathered, testing of metal, character building, turning failure into success, disaster narrowly averted, necessity to rebuild.

**Unfavorably Placed**—Storm, destruction, natural violence, accident, wreck, injury by mishap, crime of passion, impulsive attack, injury by an animal, loss of possessions, material hardship.

Upright: Unfavorable.

Inverted: Unfavorable.

Position: First place, Hagalaz aett.

Key: Hardship

# 10. Nauthiz (Nyd): Need

Transliteration: *n*
German sound value: *n*
English sound value: *n*

The necessity to endure hardship and suffering that cannot be avoided or overcome. There is no glory or victory in this endurance, only the dogged will to survive. This is a symmetrical rune, unfavorable both upright and inverted.

Literal: Suffering.

Symbolic: Dark night of the soul.

Anthropomorphic: Needy person.

Physical: Pain.

Emotional: Shock.

Mental: Determination.

Spiritual: Time of trial.

**Favorably Placed**—Endurance, stubborn will to resist, refusal to surrender, defiance of fate, escape from death, recovery from a long illness, tenacity, toughness, suffering overcome, fulfilment of a burdonsome obligation or duty.

**Unfavorably Placed**—Need, want, dire extremity, emotional or physical deprivation, loss of human dignity, suffering beyond the will to resist, taking one's medicine, failure of hope, emotional numbness, clinging to life, nakedness of the soul, starvation, exposure to the elements, torment, tortures of hell, bondage.

Upright: Unfavorable.

Inverted: Unfavorable.

Position: Second place, Hagalaz aett.

Key: Necessity.

# 11. Isa (Is): Ice

Transliteration: *i*
German sound value: *i*
English sound value: *i*

The ice of winter that locks the growing things of the Earth and the deep secret things of the sea beneath its glittering mirror. Ice allures the hapless traveler onto its easy surface and then fails under his or her feet. This is a symmetrical rune, unfavorable both upright and inverted.

Literal: Ice.

Symbolic: Mask.

Anthropomorphic: A charming deceiver.

Physical: Injury by accident.

Emotional: Attraction.

Mental: Lies.

Spiritual: False belief.

**Favorably Placed**—Glamour, infatuation, dreams of glory, glittering prizes, elusive desires, superficial beauty, beguiling words, illusions, seduction, obsessive love.

**Unfavorably Placed**—Deceit, betrayal, hidden purpose, lies, manipulation, hindering, hurtful secrets, concealed meaning, plot, ambush, unforeseen disaster, cunning, stealth.

Upright: Unfavorable.

Inverted: Unfavorable.

Position: Third place, Hagalaz aett.

Key: Entrapment.

# 12. Jera (Ger): Harvest Season

Transliteration: *j*
German sound value: *j*
English sound value: *j*

The year, but more specifically the fulfillment of the year when the fruits of the summer are gathered in. The coming full circle or turning of the wheel of the seasons. This is a symmetrical rune, favorable both upright and inverted.

Literal: Harvest.
Symbolic: Wheel of karma.
Anthropomorphic: A revolutionary.
Physical: Change of health or fitness.
Emotional: Change of affection.
Mental: Change of interest.
Spiritual: Change of belief.

**Favorably Placed**—Conditions improve, transformation, alteration, fruition, things come together, upward cycle, waiting is over, fulfillment of labor, sea change, reassessment of situation.

**Unfavorably Placed**—Setback, disappointment, small return on investment, state of confusion, hopes dashed, demotion, humbling experience, bitter harvest, reaping the whirlwind, anarchy, downward cycle.

Upright: Favorable.
Inverted: Favorable.
Position: Twelfth place, Hagalaz aett.
Key: Change.

# 13. Eihwaz (Eoh): Yew

Transliteration: *y*
German sound value: *ei* (sound between *e* and *i*)
English sound value: *ei* (sound between *e* and *i*)

The elastic, serviceable wood of the yew was used to make weapons of war, and also magical amulets of protection. The yew frequently grows in graveyards and is associated with spirits of the dead, perhaps having a protective or avertive function against the restless wandering of ghosts. It is connected with magic and the powers of the Underworld. Note that it is the thirteenth rune. This is a symmetrical rune, usually favorable both upright and inverted.

Literal: Yew tree.

Symbolic: Mysteries.

Anthropomorphic: A magician or witch.

Physical: The aura.

Emotional: Supernatural awe or dread.

Mental: Spirit communications.

Spiritual: Occultism.

**Favorably Placed**—Communication with spirits or angels, active psychic ability, a spiritual guide or teacher, a reliable weapon or instrument, magical amulet or talisman, something or someone to depend upon, a familiar spirit, your guardian angel.

**Unfavorably Placed**—Death, a funeral, ghosts, poltergeists, haunted places or buildings, dreams of the dead, occult happenings, deceiving spirits, unreliable teacher or guide in spiritual matters, a bad priest, minister, or rabbi, military disaster with loss of life, necromancy.

Upright: Favorable.

Inverted: Favorable.

Position: Fifth place, Hagalaz aett.

Key: Occult.

## 14. Perth (Peordh): Apple

Transliteration: *p*

German sound value: *p*

English sound value: *p*

The apple tree, its wood and fruit. The luscious apple is a universal symbol of luxury and indulgence in sensual pleasures. Apple wood was used to make draughts for divination and for gaming purposes, thus this rune is the rune of chance.

Literal: Apple.

Symbolic: Forbidden delights.

Anthropomorphic: A seducer.

Physical: Intoxication.

Emotional: Satisfaction.

Mental: Amusement.

Spiritual: Decadence.

Favorably Placed—Abundance, opulence, satisfaction, enjoyment, celebration, indulgence, entertainment, sensuality, socializing, parties, games of chance, alcohol, good fortune, lovemaking.

Unfavorably Placed—Excess, satiety, surfeit, revulsion, too much of a good thing, bad luck in gambling, drunkenness, lust, perverse sexuality, decadence, illicit thrills, drug addiction, gluttony, rottenness, decay.

Upright: Favorable.

Inverted: Unfavorable.

Position:  Sixth place, Hagalaz aett.

Key:  Pleasure.

## 15. Algiz (Eolh): Defense

Transliteration: *z, x*
German sound value: *z*
English sound value: *x*

A warning sign for warding off the threat of painful consequences. This rune may have originated with the gesture of the splayed human hand, or, as seems to me more likely, with the talons of the hawk. It was carried into battle as an amulet of protection.

Literal:  Warning.

Symbolic:  Taboo.

Anthropomorphic:  A guardian.

Physical:  Safety.

Emotional:  Defensive.

Mental:  Suspicious.

Spiritual:  Critical.

**Favorably Placed**—Shield, protection, defender, repulsion of evil, aid in battle, frustration of the foe, watchfulness, care, timely intervention, unbreachable defense, turning back an attack onto its source.

**Unfavorably Placed**—Danger, warning, what must be shunned, holding a threat at arm's length, the forbidden, fatal attraction, inadequate defense, hidden threat, ostracized, scapegoat, sacrificial lamb.

Upright:  Favorable.

Inverted:  Unfavorable.

Position:  Seventh place, Hagalaz aett.

Key:  Protection.

# 16. Sowelu (Sigel): Sun

Transliteration: *s*
German sound value: *s*
English sound value: *s*

The Sun with its fiery rays that strike the Earth like hammer blows to scorch and blast, but also the source of all heat and light and the giver of vitality. The instrument of the gods to cause growth or destruction. This is a symmetrical rune, favorable in both the upright and inverted position, except to those who anger the gods.

Literal: The Sun.

Symbolic: Spiritual fire.

Anthropomorphic: An agent of judgment.

Physical: Fever or stroke.

Emotional: Strong affection.

Mental: Judgment.

Spiritual: Revelation.

**Favorably Placed**—Bold action, initiative, the masterstroke, moving power, vital force, galvanizer, shattering of conceit, breaking the status quo, destroyer of inertia, decision, act of will, cutting red tape, striking to the heart, justice executed.

**Unfavorably Placed**—Nemesis, retribution, an eye for an eye, punishment for sins, paying for past mistakes, exposure of guilt, divine thunderbolt, wrath of God, skeletons fall out of the closet, vengeance, blood feud, reprisal, pitiless calling to account.

Upright: Favorable.

Inverted: Favorable.

Position: Eighth place, Hagalaz aett.

Key: Judgment.

## 17. Teiwaz (Tir): The God Tew

Transliteration: *t*
German sound value: *t*
English sound value: *t*

The god Tew or Tiw, after whom Tuesday receives its name. Originally a deity of oaths and legal contracts, in later times he became a war god renowned for his courage and honor. Warriors carried this rune into battle and cut it into their bare breasts to heighten their valor.

Literal: God of war.

Symbolic: Honor.

Anthropomorphic: A soldier.

Physical: Vigor.

Emotional: Courage.

Mental: Honesty.

Spiritual: Truth.

**Favorably Placed**—Legal matters, court actions, settlements, judgments, affairs of honor, valor, heroism, eloquent defense, persuasion, witnesses come forth, fair dealing, equitable arrangement, truth upheld.

**Unfavorably Placed**—Legal battles, protracted dispute, trickery, conflict, refusal to compromise, rejection of arbitration, delayed judgment, warfare, strife, arrogance, intolerance, clash of wills, attempt to dominate.

Upright: Favorable.

Inverted: Unfavorable.

Position: First place, Teiwaz aett.

Key: Honor.

# 18. Berkana (Beorc): Birch

Transliteration: *b*
German sound value: *b*
English sound value: *b*

The birch is the earliest tree to bud and turn green in the spring, and for this reason was used to promote fertility in livestock and in human beings. This belief is still honored when those who take saunas lash each other with birch twigs, on the pretext of stimulating the circulation.

Literal: The birch tree.

Symbolic: Sexuality.

Anthropomorphic: A lover.

Physical: Fertility.

Emotional: Desire.

Mental: Creativity.

Spiritual: Growth.

**Favorably Placed**—Fertility, desire, lovemaking, conception, creation, flow of ideas, beginning of growth, new project, inception, vital energy, rites of spring, sowing wild oats, first love, playfulness, cheer, initiation.

**Unfavorably Placed**—Passion, abandon, obsession with youth, imprudence, dangerous infatuation, uncontrolled growth, possible cancer, risk of unwanted pregnancy, sexual disease, wantonness.

Upright: Favorable.

Inverted: Unfavorable.

Position: Second place, Teiwaz aett.

Key: Fertility.

# 19. Ehwaz (Eh): Horse

**M** Transliteration: *e*
German sound value: *e*
English sound value: *e*

The necessary beast for travel over land and for making war, embodying in itself the essence of speed, power, and beauty. Horses were worshiped as messengers of the gods by the Teutons.

Literal: Horse.

Symbolic: Physical virtues.

Anthropomorphic: An agent or employee.

Physical: Beauty.

Emotional: Vanity.

Mental: Unoriginal.

Spiritual: Prophetic dreams.

**Favorably Placed**—Rapid progress, the means of transportation, medium of action, ability to leap over obstacles, advancement, grace, movement on any level, social climbing, promotion, any personal vehicle such as a car, boat, or private plane.

**Unfavorably Placed**—Haste, recklessness, blind precipitation, heedlessness, a fool rushing in, fall over a precipice, forcing the issue, tempting fate, hurried business transaction, lack of control, intoxication with speed, racing, caution thrown to the wind, an imprudent purchase.

Upright: Favorable.

Inverted: Unfavorable.

Position: Third place, Teiwaz aett.

Key: Action.

# 20. Mannaz (Man): Man

ᛗ Transliteration: *m*
German sound value: *m*
English sound value: *m*

The primordial man, Adam, who is the archetype of the human race, called Mannus by the Germans. He represents the highest powers of the human mind, those qualities that separate humanity from the beasts.

Literal: First man.

Symbolic: Mental virtues.

Anthropomorphic: A scientist.

Physical: Undeveloped.

Emotional: Controlled.

Mental: Analytical.

Spiritual: Intellectualized.

**Favorably Placed**—Intelligence, foresight, vision, creative thought, craftsmanship, invention, insight, logic, skill, ideas, plans, patterns, the method to an end, design, analysis, clear expression of purpose. An intellectual leader.

**Unfavorably Placed**—Cunning, craftiness, calculation, slyness, misdirection, slight of hand, deception, manipulation, fraud, the con-artist, trickster, illusionist, shape-changer, the wearer of masks, lies, machinations.

Upright: Favorable.

Inverted: Unfavorable.

Position: Fourth place, Teiwaz aett.

Key: Intelligence.

# 21. Laguz (Lagu): Water

ᛚ

Transliteration: *l*
German sound value: *l*
English sound value: *l*

Water in all of its bewildering variety of forms, from the salt waves of the sea to the rushing power of a mighty river to the clear coolness of a forest spring, including the hidden depths of the unconscious mind.

Literal: Water.

Symbolic: Imagination.

Anthropomorphic: A seer.

Physical: Biorhythms.

Emotional: Mood swings.

Mental: Fantasies.

Spiritual: Visions.

**Favorably Placed**—A body of water, the ocean, changeability, adaptability, receptivity, emotions, sentimentality, romantics, dreamers, poets, musicians, artistic expression, imagination, fantasies, mysteries, mediumship, passive psychic ability, the occult.

**Unfavorably Placed**—Madness, obsession, mania, melancholy, nightmares, the hidden, the submerged, deep dark secrets, the underworld, suppressed thoughts and impulses, depression, suicide, drugs, escapism, excessive sleep, catatonia, coma.

Upright: Favorable.

Inverted: Unfavorable.

Position: Fifth place, Teiwaz aett.

Key: Unconscious.

Transliteration: *ng, ing*
German sound value: *ng*
English sound value: *ng*

Ing is the name of a god of the Danes who presided over the family hearth and the productive growth of the fields. Whereas Beorc rules the conception of life, Ing rules its fulfillment. Note that Ing is half the height of most other runes, and also that it is symmetrical, which makes it favorable both upright and inverted.

|  |  |
|---:|:---|
| Literal: | God of the Earth. |
| Symbolic: | Growth. |
| Anthropomorphic: | Father or mother. |
| Physical: | Nutrition. |
| Emotional: | Stability. |
| Mental: | Slow but deep thoughts. |
| Spiritual: | Faith. |

**Favorably Placed**—The patriarch, head of the house, the home, family, simple virtues, honest work, common sense, increase in value, stability, continuity, nurturing environment, growth of children, productive employment, human warmth, love.

**Unfavorably Placed**—Toil, drudgery, domestic enslavement, family responsibilities, stress, worry about career, dissatisfaction, obsession with improving lifestyle, social climbing, pressure on children to achieve, concern about the home, budget worries, renovations to the house.

|  |  |
|---:|:---|
| Upright: | Favorable. |
| Inverted: | Favorable. |
| Position: | Sixth place, Teiwaz aett. |
| Key: | Family. |

# 23. Dagaz (Daeg): Day

■

ᛗ Transliteration: *d*
German sound value: *d*
English sound value: *d*

The light of the Sun and the period of its cycle around the Earth, with the associations of reason and order and completeness. This rune is symmetrical, and is favorable both upright and inverted.

Literal: Daylight.

Symbolic: Perfection.

Anthropomorphic: A teacher.

Physical: Good health.

Emotional: Optimism.

Mental: Understanding.

Spiritual: Wisdom.

**Favorably Placed**—Clarity, total view, shadows dispelled, answer revealed, all facts known, tying up loose ends, fulfillment of cycle, coming full circle, period of study or labor, phase of life, life span, end meeting the beginning, unit of time, reincarnation.

**Unfavorably Placed**—End of growth, finish of career, breakup of a relationship, end of the road, future uncertain, limitation, boundary, termination, enclosure, fence, wall, prison, lengthening shadows, fear of the unknown, step into darkness, possible death.

Upright: Favorable.

Inverted: Favorable.

Position: Seventh place, Teiwaz aett.

Key: Understanding.

# 24. Othila (Ethel): Homeland

Transliteration: *o*
German sound value: *o*
English sound value: *e*

The hereditary possession of a people, which can be as simple as a plot of land or a house, or as extensive as a vast nation that has endured for centuries.

|  |  |
|--:|:--|
| Literal: | Native land. |
| Symbolic: | What defines identity. |
| Anthropomorphic: | An ancestor. |
| Physical: | Hereditary illness. |
| Emotional: | Attachment to a place. |
| Mental: | Sense of identity. |
| Spiritual: | Ancestral gods. |

**Favorably Placed**—Land, deed, property, house, region of birth, native country, where the heart is, accomplishments in life, inherited talents, acquired skills, credentials, works, what has been carved out by trial or won by valor, citizenship, passport, patriotism, pride of race.

**Unfavorably Placed**—Inhospitality, homelessness, homesick, wandering, exile, loss of property, loss of passport or citizenship, lack of roots, bad habits, accumulated vices, haunting memories, prejudices, bigotry, provincial attitudes, insularity, class consciousness, clannishness, jingoism, isolationism, protectionism, the grave.

|  |  |
|--:|:--|
| Upright: | Favorable. |
| Inverted: | Unfavorable. |
| Position: | Eighth place, Teiwaz aett. |
| Key: | Home. |

# RUNES AND DICE

## ■ —— Dice Oracle of Herakles

There is no archaeological evidence that runes were ever used on conventional six-sided dice. The rune dice are my invention. In the course of writing my book *Rune Magic* I considered all the various ways the runes might be represented for the purposes of magic and divination, and decided that dice would serve as the ideal medium for quick, simple divinations. Dice are portable, durable, and easy to read at a glance. They are also very old, and were used in ancient times to divine the future.

The Greek travel writer Pausanias mentions the divination by dice that was conducted in the Temple of Herakles (Hercules) in the Achaian city of Bura. It was common for pagan temples to offer methods of divination to pilgrims seeking an answer to a difficult question. In return, the pilgrims to the temple made offerings of money, which supported the needs of the priests. Pausanias writes:

> To consult the god you pray in front of the statue, and then take dice (Herakles has an enormous number of dice) and throw four on the table. For every throw of the dice there is an interpretation written on the board.[1]

Pausanias says nothing about what may or may not have been written on the dice themselves, or what shape the dice were. It is worth noting, for our own purposes of rune dice divination using pattern matrices, that the dice were used in combination with a board. This was similar to a chess board. Each square had a prophetic message written on it. The four dice were probably cast upon the board individually, and the messages of the squares upon which they landed read in order. Cornelius Agrippa, in his *Three Books of Occult Philosophy*, adds that "all such dice were made of the bones of sacrifices."[2]

## Ancient Lore of Dice

In England, one form of dice game used unmarked dice, which were directed through a funnel onto a board divided into six sections. Each section of the board carried a number from one to six. The value of a throw was determined by the number each die landed upon, not by pips on the upper surfaces of the dice. In my judgment, the practice of marking a numbered grid on the ground and casting objects upon it to determine a value is older than the current practice of putting dots directly upon the dice. It seems likely that the dice of Herakles mentioned by Pausanias were blank.

There is a direct connection between the various forms of dice that were used in the ancient world for gambling, and the casting of lots for purposes of divination. Dice almost certainly evolved out of divine lots. For centuries dice for gambling and lots for divination in temples existed side by side. As we have seen in the case of the oracle at Bura, sometimes they were combined. One legend of Herakles relates that he used dice to win the woman Acca Larentia, who was worshiped as divine in Rome. This mythic connection between dice and the gods suggests that dice were considered to be of divine origin.

The mythical inventor of dice was the Egyptian god Thoth. Plato wrote:

> The story is that in the region of Naucratis in Egypt there dwelt one of the old gods of the country, the god to whom the bird called Ibis is sacred, his own name being Theuth. He it was that invented number and calculation, geometry and astronomy, not to speak of draughts and dice, and above all writing.[3]

Thoth is the Egyptian god of magic, whom the Greeks called Hermes Trismegistus, the supposed author of the alchemical verses known as the Emerald Tablet or Smaragdine. It is significant that the god of wisdom and magic should be the mythical inventor of dice. It further suggests that dice evolved out of temple divination by the casting of lots.

Two forms of dice games were played by the Romans—cockals or knucklebones (*ludus talorum*), and dice proper (*ludus tessararum*). They called the high throw of the dice (three sixes) an "Aphrodite." Knucklebones are probably older than dice, and thus closer in form to the lots cast or drawn for divination. The knucklebone is elongated with rounded ends, and its four sides are marked similarly to dice.

# Rune Divination of the Ancient Germans

We know almost nothing about the method used by the Teutonic tribes to divine from runes, except that it appears to have been quite simple. The Roman historian Tacitus, writing in A.D. 98, records the divination practice of cutting runes into the sides of short saplings taken from a living fruit tree, probably the apple. In important divinations that affected the entire tribe, a shaman randomly cast these saplings over a white cloth. He then invoked the gods, raised his eyes skyward, and blindly picked up three runes. The meaning of the three runes was interpreted in relation to the question. In private divinations, the father of the family concerned fulfilled the role of the shaman.

Tacitus says of the Germans: "Augury and divination by lot no people practice more diligently." This shows that the use of runes among the northern tribes was well known by the Romans, and that an important aspect of rune casting was divination.

Julius Caesar, who for propaganda purposes dictated books describing his military campaigns, mentions the casting of runes for divination twice in his *Conquest of Gaul*. One of his soldiers, Valerius Procillus, was captured by the savage Germans, who cast lots three times to decide whether he should be burned alive immediately or executed at a later time. All three times the lots, which may have been runes, fell in Procillus' favor. The other mention of the runes concerns the practice of German women casting lots in order to determine a good time for the tribe to engage in a battle. It is very interesting that the woman made this divination, not the men, because it indicates a very early connection between women and the runes.

Though there is no record of runes ever having been placed on regular dice, and used in this way for divination or gambling, it is quite probable that they were. The Germans learned to use regular dice for gaming around the time of Caesar, if not earlier, and quickly became addicted to it. Tacitus says that German barbarians were so fond of dice that after having lost everything else they would even stake their own liberty as free men on a cast, and allow themselves to be made into slaves if they lost.

It would have been a natural evolution to mark the runes upon the dice, or to mark the runes on the squares of a grid on the ground or table and cast blank dice onto these squares, in a way similar to the temple divination at Bura. Merely because we have no record of this practice is not firm evidence against it. In my opinion, the ancient combination of dice and runes is more likely than unlikely.

## Structure of the Rune Dice

Each of the four rune dice that I designed for *Rune Magic* contains a rune-pair from all three of the aettir. The placement of the runes upon the dice was not accidental. Pair-runes occupy opposite facets of the same die. They are inverted relative to each other, so that for each pair of runes one is upright and one is upside-down. This produces a circular flow of occult energy around the die when it is cast. Three such currents of force are created by the runes on each die. The currents intersect above the rune on each facet of the die at right angles, creating six energy nodes, which come into being once the die is set into motion (Figure 4.1).

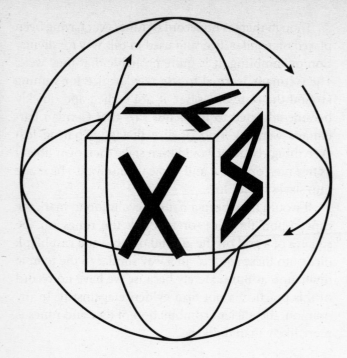

**FIGURE 4.1.** Because of the rune-pairs, occult energy flows around each die when it is cast.

Each die is a miniature model of the universe. The cube itself represents three-dimensional space. The circles of force represent the three axes of motion (up-down, right-left, back-front). Each rune-pair occupies its own axis, or spatial dimension. The six facets represent the six directions (up, down, front, back, right, left). Each time the die is cast, the rune that falls uppermost is exalted, the rune that falls under the die is suppressed, and the other four are balanced.

The cube is the three-dimensional model for our concept of reality that has been used in Western magic since ancient times. It occurs, under the guise of the six directions of space, in the oldest of all Kabbalistic books, *Sepher Yetzirah*, where the directions are linked with six abbreviated forms of the fourfold name of God, Tetragrammaton.

In describing the creation of the universe by God, the anonymous author of *Sepher Yetzirah* writes:

> *He selected three letters from among the simple ones and sealed them and formed them into a Great Name, I H V, and with this He sealed the universe in six directions.*
>
> *Fifth; He looked above, and sealed the Height with IHV.*
>
> *Sixth; He looked below, and sealed the Depth with IVH.*
>
> *Seventh; He looked forward, and sealed the East with HIV.*
>
> *Eighth; He looked backward, and sealed the West with HVI.*
>
> *Ninth; He looked to the right, and sealed the South with VIH.*
>
> *Tenth; He looked to the left, and sealed the North with VHI.*[4]

These six acts of creation follow four more fundamental actions concerning Spirit, Air, Water, and Fire, which is why these acts are numbered beginning with five. Notice that the ten actions of creation are divided into two parts, the first part with four steps and the second part with six steps. These numbers are significant, because they are the fundamental numbers of the cube, which has six square facets, each of which has four sides.

In the Enochian magic of John Dee and Edward Kelley, the four Watchtowers that stand guard at the ends of the world are arranged in the shape of a cube.[5] The cube represents the material universe, the four Watchtowers that form its sides are the boundaries of that reality and barriers against the crawling chaos that lies beyond. Each of the Watchtowers is represented by a square table. The square is the two-dimensional symbol for the material world, our familiar time-space.

The number four itself has been the numerical symbol for the physical world from the time of Pythagoras. This is why the most sacred name of God is composed of four Hebrew letters, which are transliterated IHVH. As you have seen above, the author of *Sepher Yetzirah* used permutations of the first three letters in Tetragrammaton to seal the six directions of space.

I mention these matters merely to point out how important the cube is in Western occultism, and how closely linked it is with the square and the numbers four and six. It is not a matter of minor significance to arrange the twenty-four runes in twelve pairs on the facets of four cubes. The numbers four, twelve, and twenty-four are all key numbers of Tetragrammaton, the primal Name of creation.

Tetragrammaton (IHVH) has four letters, and these letters have twenty-four permutations or arrangements, but because two of the letters are the same, only twelve distinct or overt forms of Tetragrammaton appear. Each of these twelve overt forms, called seals or (less accurately) banners, has its own shadow or occult form that is created by inverting the two identical *Hehs* in the Name. Similarly, each rune that falls uppermost when its die is cast has its own hidden pair-rune that lies under the die. These are not accidental relationships, but represent fundamental occult patterns that serve to give the rune dice immense power as a tool for both divination and practical magic.

## Polarities, Qualities, and Elements

The six runes on each die are derived from the futhark by arranging the runes in their three ancient aettir one above the other, then dividing the runes into four vertical columns, each containing three rune-pairs. It is possible to attribute each pair of runes to a polarity, an element and a quality of the zodiac using Table 4.1. Consequently, each pair of runes is linked to one of the zodiac signs.

| Aettir | Elements | | | | Qualities |
|---|---|---|---|---|---|
| | Fire | Water | Air | Earth | |
| Fehu | ᚠ ᚢ | ᚦ ᚨ | ᚱ ᚲ | ᚷ ᚹ | Fixed |
| Hagalaz | ᚺ ᚾ | ᛁ ᛃ | ᛊ ᚲ | ᛇ ᛈ | Mutable |
| Teiwaz | ᛏ ᛒ | ᛗ ᛗ | ᛚ ◊ | ᛉ ᛟ | Cardinal |
| | – + | – + | – + | – + | |
| | First Die | Second Die | Third Die | Fourth Die | |

**TABLE 4.1.** Rune correspondences.

These occult correspondences can be helpful in providing essential relationships when divining with rune dice, provided you understand the meanings of the four elements, three qualities, and two polarities. The essential meaning of each zodiac sign is based on the combination of its element, quality and polarity.

## Polarity

Positive—Expressive, spontaneous, initiatory, right side.
Negative—Repressive, receptive, reactive, left side.

## Quality

Cardinal—Enterprising, direct, linear.
Mutable—Variable, adaptable, vibratory.
Fixed—Steadfast, intense, circular.

## Elements

Fire—Expansive, energetic, spiritual.
Water—Intuitive, reflective, emotional.
Air—Interactive, mobile, intellectual.
Earth—Practical, restrained, physical.

You should look upon the polarities, qualities, and elements of the rune pairs as similar to the pattern matrices that will be described in chapters six through fifteen. They are not an organic part of the futhark, but are imposed in a rigid framework upon the three aettir, because they provide another useful level of interpretation that may be consulted when reading the rune dice during divinations.

This being understood, there are some interesting relationships between the sets of runes and their polarities, qualities, and elements. It does seem that the right rune in each pair is generally suited to the positive polarity, being more spontaneous and actively expressive, whereas the left rune is generally better suited to the negative polarity, being more reactive and repressed. This is true in most but not all of the pairs.

Similarly, it appears that the runes in the Hagalaz aett are best suited to the mutable quality, since this aett contains by far the largest number of symmetrical runes—runes whose meanings do not change when they are turned upside down. There are six symmetrical runes in the Hagalaz aett, but only one in the Fehu aett, and only two in the Teiwaz aett.

# THE PROCESS OF DIVINATION

## ■—— The Language of Symbols

Divination is often regarded merely as a way of learning future events. Predicting the future is an important part of divination, but not the whole of it. The rune dice may also be used to probe the past, to reveal hidden matters in the present, and perhaps most important of all, to chart the psychological landscape of the human mind. Through divination we are able to directly question the unconscious with the conscious, either for ourselves or for someone else.

The unconscious speaks to the conscious through a language composed of symbols common to the entire human race (which Carl Jung called *archetypes*) and personal symbols that have a specific meaning in the life of the individual. The gods of the runes are a set of archetypes which the diviner, through study, meditation, and use comes to relate to on the personal level. Each rune has a level of meaning that is universal, and

69

another level of meaning that is personal. For example, the archetypal meaning of the rune Ansuz (Os) says that Woden is the great father of both gods and the human race for everyone on Earth, but how the diviner interprets the nature of Woden depends in part on his or her personal experience with fathers. This is the personal meaning of Ansuz.

## Self-Divination

Earlier in the book I mentioned that it is easier to read the runes for someone else than it is to read them for ourselves. When we try to divine a question in our own lives, our fears, doubts, and frustration distort and exaggerate the importance of the personal aspects of the rune symbols. When we divine for someone else, it is easier to remain focused on the archetypal, or universal, significance of the runes.

The personal meanings we attach to the rune archetypes can be very useful in self-divination, but only if we are able to put them into perspective. Our unconscious can give us valuable information through these personal concepts of the rune gods provided we allow our unconscious to present its message honestly. In a self-reading, it is tempting to ignore some aspects of the runes that appear and exaggerate the importance of others, in order to slant the outcome of the reading in a way that pampers our ego and indulges our wishful fantasies. When we do readings for others, we do not care so much if their egos get a little bruised, and so, can be more honest.

I am not saying that you should never do divination for yourself, only that it is more difficult than divining for another person. If you do cast the rune dice for yourself you should bear certain general rules in mind if you wish to achieve the best results.

First, approach the divination in a serious frame of mind. Be willing to accept the judgment of the runes. Do not say to yourself, "If the runes are unfavorable, I'll just forget what they say and cast the dice again and again until I get a reading that I like." You are not only wasting your time, you are showing disrespect to the rune gods, who always know what is in your heart. They will turn their backs on you, and you will discover that you cannot get an accurate reading for either yourself or anyone else.

Second, only cast the runes when you have a question about something in your life to which you honestly need an answer. You should not cast the runes just to try them out, to amuse yourself on a slow afternoon, or to entertain your friends. The question of the reading does not need to be a major matter, but if it is about some minor event or concern in your life, it must be a matter that has personal importance to you at the time of the divination.

Third, never cast the runes for yourself or anyone else when you are frustrated, depressed, angry, miserable, hateful, afraid, sick, exhausted, or in pain. Strong negative emotions will distort your interpretations of the personal meanings of the runes in exactly the same way that exhaustion, sickness, or worry cause you to have nightmares. The same psychological mechanism is at work in both cases.

Fourth, always have your question clearly in your mind before you cast the runes. The gods of the runes cannot speak to you unless you tell them what you wish to know. One of the worst approaches to rune divination is to cast the dice with no question in mind. The runes will respond to whatever worry, bad feeling, or stress is seething below the surface of your thoughts, and you will usually find that their message is mocking or malicious.

Fifth, always know before you begin which pattern matrix you will use for the divination, and why you are using it. Different matrices serve different functions, described in the following chapters, which deal with the various forms of divination by rune dice. The type of cast you select is an important component in the outcome of the reading. If you choose a cast that is poorly suited to your question, the rune gods will not be able to communicate with you freely and the response of the runes will be less useful.

Sixth, make certain that you actually understand the runes before you attempt to cast the dice. This book provides you with basic meanings for the runes on multiple levels of reality, both microcosmically and macrocosmically, but there is much more to learn about the runes and the gods of the Teutons than was possible to fit into this book. The titles listed in the bibliography will guide you to many valuable sources of information. You should not stop with them, but continue to study the runes and the northern gods at every opportunity.

In addition, you should spend some time each day contemplating an individual rune until you are certain that you actually know the futhark yourself, not merely remember details about it from reading books. It is one thing to be able to rattle off the names and definitions of the runes by rote; it is more valuable to understand the living identities of the runes on the intuitive level.

## Divining for Others

When you cast the runes for another person, it is best if you know as much as possible about his or her circumstances and personalities. Some psychics and fortune tellers maintain that it is better to know nothing about a querent, not even the question of the reading. In their view, a good diviner will learn everything needed during the divination itself. However, the more you know about the querent, and why he or she has come to you for a reading, the more precisely you will be able to interpret the runes. A rune on a pattern matrix has numerous possible shades of meaning when considered in itself, but only one precise interpretation when placed in the context of a specific question. The object of this background information is not to deceive the querent, but to narrow down the possible meanings of a cast.

Spend some time before the reading getting to know the querent and his or her situation. Discuss the question that is to serve as the basis for the reading. This will fix the question in both your mind and the mind of the querent. It is useful to have the querent write the question out on a piece of paper, because it ensures that the question is clear and concise. If you find that the question is vague or too complicated, encourage the querent to simplify it. At most, it should contain no more than a dozen words or so, and must always be specific. The many subtle shades of meaning and the complex web of details that surround the question will come out during the reading.

You may discover that it is easier to get accurate readings for strangers than for friends or family members. Friends and family are an extension of the perceived self (what you believe yourself to be, as opposed to what you truly are, the true self). When casting the runes for a friend, you often run into the same problem encountered when casting for yourself. Emotions, memories, and desires can distort your interpretation of the runes.

The only way to overcome this difficulty is to place yourself in an altered frame of mind while casting the runes. Cease to view yourself as a friend or relative of the querent, and instead perceive yourself in the role of an impartial interpreter. Tell yourself that you are there merely to report the message of the rune gods as accurately as possible. This will help you to gain some distance from your emotions and improve the likelihood of a true reading.

If your relative or friend refuses to take you seriously, and scoffs or jokes about the runes, stop the reading at once. It will produce no useful result, and will very likely injure your own relationship with the rune gods, making future readings less productive.

Never do a reading at a social gathering where more than one or two other persons are present, and never do a reading for an individual who has been drinking or is high on drugs. These situations encourage an attitude of disrespect. It is hard to resist the urging of friends and family, who will wish you to perform with the dice for their amusement. If you give in to this social pressure, you will regret it later when you attempt to use the runes for any serious purpose.

## Professional Divination

The rune dice make an excellent tool for professional diviners who wish to use the runes for a quick and precise reading. They are a valuable supplement to rune wands, rune cards, and rune stones, but they possess enough depth of meaning that they can be the primary instrument of divination by runes.

A few words should be said about the ethics of casting the runes for money. When I divine, I take no money and accept no gifts. I divine for myself infrequently, and refuse to cast the runes merely to amuse or satisfy the curiosity of friends and family members. I have made a personal decision that it would be disrespectful to use rune divination as a source of income or amusement. However, I have no wish and no power to impose this view on the rest of the world. If you use the rune dice professionally, and are paid for your services, I merely ask that you charge a modest fee and behave in an honorable manner. Do not try to abuse the runes, or you will regret it.

When interpreting a rune cast, it is almost impossible not to express personal opinions or give advice that you believe may be helpful to the querent. However, it is good practice to make a distinction between what the runes are saying to you and what conclusions you draw from their message in relation to the life circumstances of the querent.

You should preface any advice you give with words such as "In my opinion...," "My conclusion would be...," or "I would respond this way...." Try to make it clear to the querent where the message of the runes ends and your own editorial commentary begins. Usually the querent will be anxious to hear your counsel, but in the end it is up to the querent how he or she responds to the message of the runes.

## Making the Rune Dice

This book comes with its own set of dice, but if for some reason you need to make other dice, you can do so quite easily. Obtain two sets of large ordinary plastic dice. Make sure they have sharp corners—some dice have rounded corners and are not suitable. Cut twenty-four squares out of white adhesive labels so that the squares are slightly smaller than the sides of the dice.

Peel off the backs of the labels and stick the squares to the four dice. Use a red pen to mark the twenty-four runes on the labels on the sides of the dice. It is important to use red ink whenever you draw the runes.

It is not enough merely to mark them on the correct dice; there is a specific and important pattern to the runes. They must be in the proper order relative to each other. As I said earlier, pair-runes are placed on opposite facets of each die, and one is inverted to create a circular current of force. The illustration on the following page shows the rune dice opened out flat into crosses with the runes marked on them in such a way that when the crosses are folded together into cubes, the runes will assume the correct relationship to each other (Figure 5.1). You may wish to actually draw

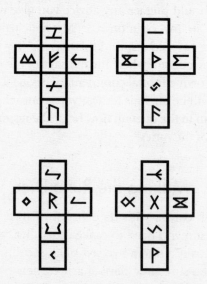

**FIGURE 5.1.** The runes are marked so that when the crosses are folded together as cubes, the runes will assume the correct relationships to one another.

these crosses on a piece of paper, cut them out, and fold them into cubes. In this way you will be absolutely sure to draw the runes on the proper facets of your dice, and in the proper attitudes.

## The Pattern Matrices

The pattern matrices for the different rune casts described in this book are all quite simple. They are easy to remember, and simple to draw or mark on any flat surface. They may be scratched on the ground with a stick, drawn on a concrete floor with chalk, or sketched on a large sheet of paper with a pencil or pen. You may either draw them ahead of time and store them away to reuse over and over, or draw each matrix afresh just before casting the dice.

A convenient size for the pattern matrices is from eighteen to twenty-four inches. The best size will be determined by your manner of casting the dice. The dice should not roll off the matrix on which they are cast, but this is not absolutely essential. All the matrices radiate from a central point, and you can imagine their patterns extending beyond the edges of the drawing. If one of the dice happens to roll off the drawing, by mentally extending its lines you can still accurately read the rune on the die. If you gently cast the dice close to the matrix, they will not spread widely and you will be able to use a smaller matrix. If you drop the dice from a greater height they will roll farther, and you will find that you need a larger matrix to keep all the dice within its boundaries.

A cheap and convenient way to make the matrix for a cast is to draw it on an opened double sheet of newspaper with a wide felt-tipped marker or crayon. The paper can be discarded once the reading is over. Select a sheet that has mostly fine print on it, so that the matrix will stand out from the background.

Professional diviners may prefer to buy large sheets of white paper. It provides an extra element of interest in a reading by drawing the matrix for a cast yourself right in front of the querent, who will probably ask you to explain what it means. This helps to establish a good rapport with the querent, and if the querent is a stranger, serves to break the ice.

An alternative is to construct the pattern matrices ahead of time and store them in a safe place until they are needed. This makes it possible to use more expensive materials, such as hardboard or fabric, and to paint the matrices more elaborately using the appropriate colors (which are described for each matrix). If you plan to frequently or exclusively use a single matrix, or several matrices, and intend to do many readings, this is probably the best course to follow. The borders of the matrices may be decorated with runes or other appropriate symbols. This does not increase the effectiveness of the matrices, but renders them more appealing to the eye, a consideration important to professional diviners.

## Beginning a Reading

In conducting a reading of the runes, talk to the querent for a few minutes to learn something about the person and his or her area of interest. Make sure that you have the querent voice the question just before sitting down at the table, or better still, just before you cast the runes. The closer the question is asked to the casting of the runes, the fresher it will be in both your mind and the mind of the querent. It is not a bad idea to have the querent write the question down on a slip of paper at the table, and to keep the written question on the table during the reading.

Readings are best conducted on a square table. Seat the querent on one side and sit on the opposite side. The table should be small enough for you to easily clasp the hands of the querent. This allows personal contact during the reading, which can be comforting to the querent. If the matrix is pre-drawn, it will already be on the table. If you intend to draw it yourself, the table will hold a large new sheet of paper and a marking instrument of some kind. The paper should be white, with the line left by the marker black or nearly so. If the matrix is drawn on newspaper, use an uncolored sheet—white and black are neutral colors, and will not bias the reading. Pre-drawn natrices may be either black and white, or tinted in their appropriate colors. It is better if the line of the matrix is drawn very distinct and thick. An artist's charcoal stick works well, as does a black felt pen or a pencil with a soft, oversized lead.

Draw the matrix, take the rune dice out of their case or pouch. Extend them on the palms of your two joined hands, and have the querent gently blow on them. (When you do divination for yourself, you should hold the dice in your own hands and blow on them.) The breath is the vehicle of the spirit. The practice of blowing on dice for luck is ancient and magically correct. It is equivalent to allowing the querent to shuffle the cards in a Tarot reading. The breath of the querent creates a physical link between the querent and the runes, and serves to focus his or her mind on the question. Instruct the querent to keep the question in mind while blowing on the dice.

# Invocation to Woden

Just before making a cast, it is useful to mentally express a brief prayer of invocation to Woden, the father of humankind and the mythic discoverer of the runes. In expressing the invocation, you allow yourself to become Woden for the purpose of the reading, just as the ancient Teutonic shamans became Woden when they received the wisdom of the runes.

Fold your hands together around the dice by closing them upward so that your two thumbs touch, then press your hands over your heart-center (the center of your chest). Either shut your eyes or elevate your gaze heavenward while you silently voice the prayer. If you wish, the prayer may be spoken aloud, but make sure you know it perfectly before you try to speak it. An original invocation composed by you for your own use will have greater personal power, provided you understand how such a prayer should be constructed. You may prefer to use the following prayer:

> *All-Father, Soul-flyer,*
> *Single-seer, Far-walker,*
> *Fair-speaker, Spear-shaker,*
> *Tree-rider, Rune-maker.*
>
> *Guide these hands true to cast,*
> *Guide these eyes true to see,*
> *Guide this mind true to read,*
> *Guide this mouth true to speak.*
>
> *By Sleipnir's hoof, so let it be,*
> *By Suttung's mead, so let it be,*
> *By Gungnir's shaft, so let it be,*
> *By Fenrir's jaw, so let it be.*

The references in the prayer are to important elements in the myth of Woden. Knowledge of these matters gives the speaker power over the god. Sleipnir was Woden's horse, upon whose teeth runes were carved, and whose legs numbered the same number of runes in an aett. Suttung was the giant from whom Woden stole the dwarf-mead of poetic speech. Gungnir was Woden's dwarf-forged spear, which the god used to gash himself while suspended from Yggdrasill (a word which means "the horse of Woden"). Fenrir was the ferocious giant wolf that killed Woden during Ragnarök, the Doom of the Gods.

Woden was called the One-eyed because he plucked out one of his own eyes and gave it to Mimir, the wisest of the gods, as a pledge in return for a drink from the well of wisdom. He was known as Road-practiced because he was in the habit of walking the Earth in the disguise of an old man. He was called Eagle-headed because he could change himself into an eagle and take flight. He was known as Gungnir's-shaker after his famous dwarf spear. He was called All-father because he was the father of gods and men.

The invocation to Woden is not absolutely necessary in divining with runes. If you feel uncomfortable about the prayer, omit it. However, it is useful in establishing a connection in the mind between the question of the divination and the source of occult potency that will reveal the answer to the question, the gods of the runes. The prayer reminds us what the runes are and where they originated. By symbolically becoming Woden we take on Woden's knowledge and skill in the use of runes.

## Casting the Runes

After invoking the presence of Woden, cup your two hands together to create a hollow space with the dice still between them. Shake your hands to mix the dice, then hold them out together over the pattern matrix and open them at the bottom (where your little fingers meet) so that the dice fall onto the middle of the matrix and spread evenly. I have found that when I cast the dice using both hands by dropping them straight down onto the matrix, their distribution tends to be more even than when I cast them using one hand.

Do not hold your hands so high that the dice roll off the edge of the paper. If one or two of the dice do happen to roll beyond the boundary of the matrix, you should still be able to read them by mentally extending the lines of the matrix, which will place these rogue dice within one of its zones. In the event that a die rolls too far away to be read, or rolls completely off the table, begin the reading all over again by having the querent blow once more across the dice and repeating the invocation to Woden.

## Divination Is Only One Function of the Runes

The term "casting the runes" is sometimes also applied to the practice of projecting the occult forces of the runes onto a specific person, place, object, or circumstance during ritual magic. Divination is only one function of runes. They were used for many other purposes in ancient times. Methods for sending the runes to accomplish willed purposes by magical means are described in chapter seventeen. In this book, which mainly concerns divination by rune dice, the term "casting" is used exclusively to signify the cast of the dice. The projection of the powers of the runes in magic is here called "sending."

# SKY MATRIX CAST

## ■——— The Circle Is the Symbol of the Universe

The Sky Matrix is a blank surface with no divisions. The runes on the dice are read strictly in relation to one another, with no reference to any external pattern. When cast, the dice create their own pattern, and this pattern changes from one cast to the next. It is not really necessary to use a physical pattern matrix when employing this cast.

If you wish, you can represent the Sky Matrix with a large, empty circle drawn or marked on any convenient flat surface. Paint or color the inside of the circle sky blue if you decide to make a permanent Sky Matrix pattern (Figure 6.1).

The circle is the symbol of the universe. It contains everything. The circle should be conceived as infinitely large. Like the universe, it has no outside. Even if a die rolls outside the physical circle you have drawn, it is

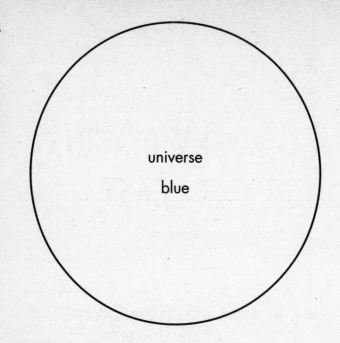

**FIGURE 6.1.** The Sky Matrix.

considered to still remain within the circle for the purposes of the reading.

The four runes that fall uppermost on the dice are interpreted according to basic principles of divination. These principles are universal and may be applied to any form of divination that uses the random fall or positioning of objects. The dice are read from the perspective of the diviner, in relation to the diviner and to each other. Neither the querent nor any other external references are considered. The diviner represents the center point of the universe. The dice create their own simple two-dimensional model of reality when they fall in relation to the diviner.

# Distance

Nearness in space equals nearness in time. The rune that falls closest to the diviner pertains to the foundation of the present, the next farther out has to do with the present situation, the next rune with the near future evolving out of the present, and the most distant rune relates to the distant future of the matter under question. The nearest rune may also pertain to past events that are relevant to the reading, since the past exists in the present moment via memory and other forms of karma.

It is sometimes convenient to think of the nearest rune as the past, the two middle runes as the present, and the farthest rune as the future. However, this is a simplistic way of regarding the cast. Past, present, and future are contained and expressed in each of the runes. Their distance from the diviner merely indicates the relative importance of the time factors.

The nearest rune bears most on the events that influenced the present situation. Since it is the closest rune, it shows the earliest seminal influences. These are usually deep in the past, but may still continue to exist in the present and may extend themselves into the future. Similarly, the farthest rune from the diviner shows the factors that resolve or answer the question. These usually express themselves in the future, but they may also exist in the present or past.

If there is an unequal separation in distance of the rune dice from the diviner, it indicates an unequal division of time. For example, say a single rune is close to the diviner, but is separated by a large space from the three remaining runes, which are clumped together on the far side of the gap. This positioning suggests an immediate event that will have important repercussions in the distant future. It also indicates a significant lapse of time between the start and the conclusion of the matter. Three runes grouped together near the reader with a single rune farther away indicates that the question will be resolved immediately or very soon, but will have an unforeseen effect in the more distant future.

A more or less equal spacing of the runes, in terms of distance from the diviner, shows that the matter under question will unfold gradually over time. If the rune dice form a line or arc and are all approximately the same distance away from the diviner, this indicates that the question of the reading will resolve itself immediately or very shortly without any unforeseen consequences in the more distant future.

## Left and Right

The left side of the diviner is read as the left side of the querent because during the reading the diviner acts as the agent for the querent. The left side, from the perspective of the diviner, is associated with secrets yet to be revealed and wishes or desires unfulfilled. It may also indicate something that will be done to the querent, happen to the querent, or be given to the querent. It may indicate a meeting or visit by someone who comes to the querent. The matters represented by runes on the left are more likely to be private or hidden, and have psychological or emotional consequences. In magic the left is the receptive side.

The right side, from the perspective of the diviner, signifies communications and actions that will be taken by the querent. In magic, the right side is the side of projection. What is on the right side will occur in public in plain view. It will have material consequences. Runes on the right may indicate travel by the querent, and new experiences of a physical and social nature.

Three runes to the left and one to the right suggests that the matter of the question will unfold itself predominately in a private or a psychological way. The querent will be the observer and reactor to events, not the prime mover. Three runes on the right and one on the left indicates that the matter under question involves events that lie outside the querent and his or her immediate surroundings, and that the querent will bring about the conclusion of the matter by some overt action. Two runes on the left and two runes on the right shows that the question will be resolved in a balanced way with equal give and take.

## Contact

When two dice touch or come very close to touching, their runes act in unison. A pair of rune dice in contact may stand for lovers, friends, or a married couple. It may mean an important or intimate meeting with an individual.

Three runes in contact, or nearly touching, suggest that events will come to a head and resolve themselves very rapidly. Whether this resolution takes place in the near or distant future depends on whether this trine is closest to the diviner or farthest away. This is determined by the relative position of the fourth die. If the fourth die is nearer the diviner than the group of three, the resolution will occur in the more distant future. If the fourth die is farther away than the three that are clustered, the resolution will occur soon. If the fourth die is approximately the same distance away from the diviner as the three dice that touch, the resolution will be in the middle distance, neither early nor late. Three runes touching may also stand for a child, a family, or a small social gathering.

Four runes touching or very near to each other—an extremely unusual occurrence—suggests some event that will radically change the life of the querent. This might be something like the winning of a lottery or the death of a family member, depending on how favorable or unfavorable the runes are. Four runes touching sometimes indicates a large social gathering of great importance. The exact interpretation will depend on the question.

It is not necessary for the dice to be in actual physical contact to regard them as touching. If the dice are separated by less than their own dimension, they may be considered to be in contact. Dice that are three-quarters of an inch square would be said to touch provided they fell less than three-quarters of an inch apart.

This interpretation is similar to the use of orbs in astrology. The function of orbs is to determine aspects between planets when the planets do not form perfect angles, which is usually the case. If astrologers were forced to wait until the planets were in perfect trine, square, or sextile aspects, very few aspects would appear in charts. Similarly, it is quite unusual for two or three rune dice to fall in actual physical contact, but not so uncommon for a pair of rune dice, or even three, to fall very near each other. Even if they are not in physical contact, four dice falling closely together in a cast is unusual.

## Lines

When the dice fall into a more or less straight line, the matter under question will proceed in a simple and direct way to its resolution, without complications or delays. The direction of progress is indicated by the distance of the runes from the diviner. The nearest rune expresses itself first, followed by the second, third, and fourth. When the dice form a line, the action of each rune after the first depends on and flows out from the rune that precedes it in time. The runes form links in a chain of cause and effect. None can act independently of the others.

Sometimes the dice form a smooth arc. This indicates an influence affecting the action of the runes. The direction of the outer bulge of the curve is the direction of influence. This may be imagined as similar to a magnet pulling on a wire from the side and causing it to bend toward the magnet. Curves that bulge to the left show the prevailing influence of something secret or hidden. Curves that bulge to the right suggest the importance of some visible physical object, place, or structure. Curves that bulge toward the diviner reveal an underlying past influence. Curves that bulge away from the diviner show that some future factor not a part of the runes themselves will determine the matter.

When the dice fall into a zigzag pattern, this suggests that the matter of the divination will have a number of surprising twists and turns before it reaches its final outcome. There may be blind alleys and false starts along the way. How important these will be is suggested by the sharpness of the angles in the zigzag.

It should be understood that you will almost never get a perfectly straight line, a perfect curve, or a perfectly symmetrical zigzag line when you cast the runes. You must use judgment and intuition when deciding where one type of line ends and another type begins. When the runes form a line that is partly curved and partly zigzag, for example, both the curve and the zigzag apply to it in a mixed degree. One or the other tendency will usually dominate.

# Triangles

Three of the dice in a cast often form the figure of a triangle. Indeed, any three dice will always form a triangle in the strict sense of the word unless they fall along a perfectly straight line. For this reason, it is best to limit the definition of a triangular figure in rune divination to triangles that are approximately equilateral—that have lines of more or less equal lengths. This excludes from consideration the vast majority of triangular figures that are narrow and elongated. Sometimes the dice form two nearly equilateral triangles that share the same base. When this happens, each should be considered separately as an independent entity, even though both share two runes in common.

An equilateral triangle in a cast is a favorable figure that influences the entire course of the matter under question. It indicates harmony and order, and points to a positive outcome. Events will unfold in the querent's favor, and he or she will experience good luck. The three runes in a triangle are mutually dependent on each other. Each has a direct influence on the other two. They must be considered as a group.

A right triangle, which is a tringle with one angle of ninety degrees, is unbalanced. The rune that lies at this ninety-degree corner is the focus of the other two runes on the acute angles. These two runes exert conflicting influences on the rune at the ninety-degree corner. The closer rune exerts the strongest pull, and has the greatest influence.

When a triangle appears in a cast, the fourth rune will have one of three relationships with the triangle. If the fourth rune is inside the triangle, it represents the heart of the matter around which everything else turns. It is the fulcrum or pivot—by concentrating his or her resources on the thing this rune represents, the querent can control the development and outcome of the matter.

If the fourth rune is opposite one of the sides of the triangle, it defines that side as the base of the triangle. The fourth rune signifies the foundation or root of the matter, the source from which the whole matter springs. This may be concealed, and often, but not always, lies in the past. The root of the matter may also be the future fulfillment of some desire or dream. By analyzing it the querent can better understand the origin of the situation. If this fourth rune opposite the side of the triangle happens to be the rune farthest from the diviner, it suggests that the foundation of the matter will only become manifest in the future at the outcome of everything to do with the question.

If the fourth rune is opposite one of the points of the triangle, it defines that point as the apex of the triangle. The fourth rune then stands for the outcome or fulfillment of the matter under question. It is the focus to which everything that has gone before flows. Picture it as though the triangle were the head of an arrow pointing toward this fourth rune. Usually this fourth rune represents something that will occur in the future, and in plain view of everyone. However, when the fourth rune opposite the point of the triangle is the rune nearest the diviner, it may mean that the answer or solution to the question has already occurred, but has not yet been discovered by the querent.

It must be understood that the runes seldom are so cooperative as to fall into the shape of an exact equilateral triangle, or precisely in the center or opposite the points of such a triangle. You must use your judgment in determining when the fourth rune lies off a point of the triangle, and when it is opposite one of the sides. You must also decide how much deviation from a perfect equilateral figure you will allow in your reading yet still regard the figure as a triangle. The more distorted the triangle, the less harmonious and cohesive its action. Beyond a certain point the runes act independently.

A good rule of thumb is to look at the dice when you cast them, and if a regular triangle immediately seems to jump out at you, you have a triangle. If, on the other hand, you must make an effort to see a triangular figure in the pattern of the dice, you probably do not have a viable triangle. Very elongated or distorted triangles, and those triangles that have angles greater than ninety degrees (obtuse angles) should be ignored. The more regular the triangular figure, the more importance it has in the reading.

## Squares

Sometimes the dice fall into a pattern that approximates a square. This is seldom perfect. The same rule of thumb that I gave for distinguishing triangles applies to squares. If the shape of a square is obvious in a cast, you have a square. If you must make allowances for unequal angles and lines, you probably do not have a viable square figure. A viable figure is one that exerts a significant influence on the matter under inquiry.

Squares are unfavorable. They indicate an unsatisfactory or unhappy course for the entire matter. The nearer to perfect the square figure is, the more unfortunate its influence. I use the term "influence" here in the same sense that it is used in astrology. Square figures in a cast do not actually influence anything—they merely reflect an unfortunate set of circumstances affecting the matter under question.

A square in a cast signifies division and conflict. Sometimes the querent can react to this situation as a challenge and through great effort overcome it. Squares test the character of the querent. If the querent is strong-willed, they can be met head-on and defeated; if the querent is weak, a square may prove disastrous. In either case, the appearance of a well-shaped square in a cast points to a rough road ahead for the querent. If the square is distorted, its harmful power is mitigated.

## Sky Matrix, Sample Cast

A young woman becomes pregnant, and she wants to know whether she should get married.

She is a university student with one more year remaining in an arts degree. Her grades were good, but recently have begun to suffer. She is considering taking a year off to have her child, with the intention of resuming her schooling at a later date, perhaps on a part-time basis. Her lover proposed marriage after learning of her condition. They have been seeing each other for a little more than seven months. He recently found work as an assistant manager in a computer store.

Figure 6.2 (page 94) shows how the dice in the querent's Sky Matrix cast fell. The cast revealed the following factors.

The nearest rune is Perth (Peordh), which signifies intoxication and sensual enjoyment. It stands for the love affair. Obviously the querent is head over heels in love. This should sound a cautionary note, since infatuation interferes with rational judgment.

The next closest rune to the diviner is Mannaz (Man), which may represent the lover in this cast. Since Perth is the left of these two runes, the sensual delight it signifies is probably that enjoyed by the querent (the left side points to things received or experienced). Mannaz also stands for intellect, and in the context of the

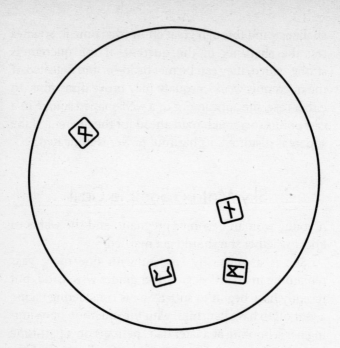

**FIGURE 6.2.** The fall of the dice in the Sky Matrix sample cast.

question, the querent's higher education. The two runes, Perth and Mannaz, are the two poles of the magnet that tug the querent in opposite directions.

Next in distance is the rune Nauthiz (Nyd). This always signifies suffering or hardship. Since it is located directly above the rune Mannaz, and is on the right side of the cast, one interpretation is that the suffering will be borne mainly by the man, and will be of an external type, perhaps financial or social hardship. It may signify that the man will choose to carry the burden of hardship in the relationship. However, if we interpret Mannaz as the university studies of the querent, Nauthiz above it indicates that achieving a degree will be difficult for her and will require endurance and persistence.

The outermost rune in distance from the diviner is Othila (Ethel), which means native land or homeland. It is a significant distance apart from the other three runes, and far to the left. This is probably the happy home and family that the querent nurtures in her wishes and dreams as the ultimate fulfillment of her pregnancy. Its separation from the other runes indicates that it is still a distant goal, and more of a dream than a reality.

The three runes Perth, Mannaz, and Nauthiz form a right-angle triangle. This shows that these three influences are bound together. Because the triangle is far from regular, the interaction is not very harmonious or beneficial. It is a right-angle triangle, so therefore the rune that falls on the right-angled corner is influenced separately by the runes on the two outer acute angles, which tend to pull it in two different directions. Mannaz as the querent's education is torn between sensual and emotional indulgence and the hardship of self-denial and study.

Alternatively, Mannaz as the querent's lover is pulled between his love for the querent and his awareness of the hardship that looms in his future. Since the lover did not propose marriage until after learning of the pregnancy, we might suspect that he is aware of the rough road ahead but is willing to make a sacrifice for the querent because of his love for her. Notice that the Nauthiz rune of suffering and hardship is closer to the Mannaz rune than the Perth rune of sensual delight, and so exerts the greater influence.

The fourth rune, Othila, lies opposite the side of the triangle defined by the Perth and Nauthiz runes. These define a line that separates the distant Othila rune on the left side of the cast, the side of dreams and wishes, from the Mannaz rune on the right side, the side of material reality. Othila is thus at the base of the question, but because it is the farthest rune from the diviner it will not show itself until the more distant future.

My interpretation of this cast is that the happy home the querent fantasizes about does not lie in her immediate circumstances. It is a dream rather than a probable reality, at least at this stage in her life. Her immediate future, in connection with her lover and her education (Mannaz), will be one of trial and hardship that will test her endurance. In about twice the time it takes her to complete her education she will be at the stage when she can seriously contemplate a settled home and family.

The querent should stay in school, and draw on the love and resources of her boyfriend for help in taking care of her child while she works hard to obtain her degree. If all goes well, she will be ready to get married in two years or so.

# SUN MATRIX CAST

## ■————— Inside and Outside

The Sun Matrix divides the circle of the universe into two zones—inside and outside. The smaller inner circle is colored black and the large outer circle is yellow (Figure 7.1, page 98). The outer circle should be conceived of as infinite in dimension. If, during a cast, one of the dice happens to roll outside the large, outer circle as it is physically drawn on the paper, merely extend its boundary in your mind so that the rogue die rests within it.

Strictly speaking, all you need for this cast is the smaller inner circle. The outer circle is everything else in the universe. The inner circle can be represented by a small circle scratched in the ground, or by a disk of paper or some other convenient material. You may need to experiment with its size. It should be just large enough so that when you cast the dice on it, on average over the course of dozens or hundreds of throws half

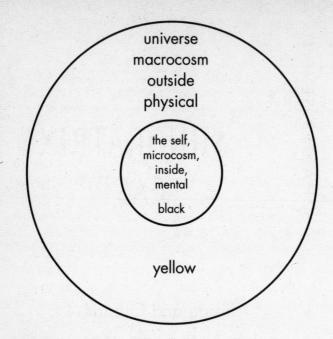

**FIGURE 7.1.** The Sun Matrix.

the time half the dice fall outside its limit. A circle of four to six inches is about right for gentle casts close to the surface of the table.

As an alternative to drawing the small circle on paper, you may wish to experiment with a saucer or other small plate. This gives a more graphic impression of the distinction between inside and outside. When the dice are cast into a saucer with just the right force, some of them will stay in the saucer and some will bounce out. You do not want all the dice staying inside the saucer, but neither do you want all of them going out of the saucer.

Once you find the right size for the inner circle it does not matter if from time to time all the dice stay inside the circle, or all the dice roll out of it. This

unusual result for a cast should be considered as a   99
legitimate part of the reading.

■

SUN MATRIX CAST

## Model of the Universe

This division of reality into inside and outside takes precedence over all other relationships and patterns that may be formed between the dice and the diviner, or among the dice themselves. Indicators such as distance from the diviner, contact between dice, triangles, squares, and lines still apply, but they are secondary in consideration to whether a particular die comes to rest inside or outside the small circle. This pattern matrix should be understood as a very simple model of the universe that reduces the complexity of our reality down to very simple terms—in this case, in and out.

The Sun Matrix gives insight into the nature and identity of the querent in the context of a particular question. It is best used to investigate attitudes, responses, thoughts, and feelings. The small circle symbolizes the wholeness of the querent on a personal level, while the large circle stands for the wholeness of the universe. Inside the small circle is the microcosm; outside the small circle is the macrocosm. This is a good matrix to use for questions that deal with the way the querent is functioning, or failing to function, in the larger world. It yields valuable advice about the balancing of personality and the successful integration of the self.

On a physical level this matrix can reveal important factors that relate to the immune system, general vitality, and the heart and the circulatory system. On the emotional level it often shows matters that concern the attitude held by the querent toward humanity at large, and the querent's ability to confront and deal with other individuals. On the mental level it reveals how the querent views him or herself in relation to the world. On the spiritual level it provides information about the querent's moral beliefs and concept of God. This is the most intensely personal of all the pattern matrices. It is best used as a mirror in which the querent can be made to see his or her own prejudices, conceits, weaknesses, and virtues.

## Sun Matrix, Sample Cast

A young man wishes to know whether he should seriously consider a career in the army.

His high school grades are average. He has no firm conviction about what he should do with the rest of his life, and career counseling has been of little help. He has no money saved, and his parents are unwilling to pay for his university tuition. He hopes that a few years as a soldier will give him a goal for the future and make him into a more mature and self-reliant person.

When cast upon the Sun Matrix, the runes took the pattern shown in Figure 7.2.

Only one die has remained inside the circle of the microcosm. The rune upon it, Fehu (Feoh), represents the significant feature of the querent's personality. The other three runes are factors of the larger world that have a bearing on this quality in the querent's nature within the context of the question.

Fehu is the rune that means cattle. By extension it indicates subservience, timidity, lack of freedom, and an inability to make bold, independent decisions. Cattle are possessions owned by someone else. This is the view the querent holds about himself. He believes that he is not in control of his own life, that he is being herded through a system that is indifferent to his personal desires or needs.

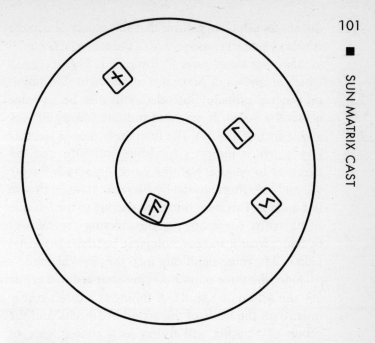

**FIGURE 7.2.** The fall of the dice in the Sun Matrix sample cast.

The extreme degree of imbalance in the position of the single rune in the circle of the microcosm points to an imbalance in the personality of the querent. He is very badly out of touch with his own center. It is located at the bottom of the circle, suggesting a low self-esteem, and a general sense of hopelessness and depression.

The nearest to the diviner of the three runes that fell outside the circle of the microcosm is Sowelu (Sigel), the lightning stroke of heavenly judgment. This is an unforgiving rune. It punishes mistakes and weaknesses without pity. Its action is usually violent. Since it is located on the right side of the cast, this violence will take a physical rather than a psychological form of expression. Sowelu is approximately the same distance from the diviner as Fehu, suggesting that the action of Sowelu comes as a direct consequence of the action of Fehu.

The next outer rune in distance is Laguz (Lagu), which means water. Since it is on the right side, physical water is probably intended. This may be a voyage across the ocean. It may also indicate some glittering and seductive illusion. The final outer rune is Nauthiz (Nyd), which indicates hardship, suffering, and the necessity to endure. Nauthiz especially stands for the toil and suffering endured by a servant, slave, or person in bondage. This rune is located slightly to the left side of the matrix, suggesting that the suffering it reveals will be both physical and psychological, but that the mental pain will be more significant than the physical pain.

Since the three outer runes are arranged in a gentle arc, the action of Laguz will follow as a direct consequence on the heels of the action of Sowelu, and the action of Nauthiz will follow as a consequence of Laguz. The curve bends toward the right side. This shows that the matter of the reading is governed or influenced by some material, overt consideration.

My interpretation of this cast is that the querent has an extremely low opinion of his own abilities and worth as a human being, and that he has not yet discovered himself. The judgment of the rune Sowelu is probably the consequence that will befall him as a result of his poor attitude and confusion about his true identity and rightful place in the world. In the context of the question, Sowelu represents the living hell of basic training that the querent will suffer as a direct result of his inability to decide what to do with his life.

Laguz on the right indicates a sea voyage, which suggests that the querent will sign up for the navy or some sea-going branch of the military. He will probably be sent overseas on a military assignment. Nauthiz as the final most distant rune shows that he will be extremely unhappy during his term of service. He may also be wounded or fall sick.

The three runes Fehu, Laguz, and Nauthiz form a fairly regular triangle, but in this particular case the harmonizing effects of the triangular figure are negated by the negative runes that compose it. Reading these three runes together by distance, we get weakness, illusion, and suffering. The foundation rune that lies opposite the base of the triangle, Sowelu, indicates that this negative cycle of emotion is experienced as a result of natural law, or the personal karma of the querent. He is following the path of least resistance that will lead to disaster like a cow that allows itself to be led to the slaughterhouse.

The other triangle—Fehu, Sowelu, and Lagu—is less regular, and therefore a less significant influence in the reading as a whole. It is on the right side of the cast, indicating physical matters. Here, when the runes are read in order of distance, the cycle is blind obedience (Fehu), judgment from above (Sowelu), and a sea voyage (Laguz). The obedience of the querent to his superiors leads him to obey their orders to embark overseas. The foundation rune of the second triangle is Nauthiz, indicating that suffering and the need to endure is at the bottom of the querent's obedience to authority.

My advice to the querent is that he would be foolish to even consider enlisting in the military, since he is tempted to join the armed services only because he has a low opinion of his own worth and does not know what to do with his life now that he has finished high school. He hopes to delay the necessity to make a decision about his future by letting others control his thoughts and actions for several years. Instead of enlisting, the querent should seek career and psychological counseling, and make a strong effort to focus on a definite goal in life that is in harmony with his interests and innate talents.

# MOON MATRIX CAST

## Dark and Light

The Moon Matrix pattern is a model of the universe that divides everything into left and right. It is represented by a large circle with a vertical line down its center. The left half of the circle is colored black, and the right half is colored white or silver (Figure 8.1, page 106). The circle of the matrix should be conceived as infinitely large. If during a cast one of the dice happens to roll outside its boundary, merely extend the middle line up or down in your mind until the rogue die rests on the left or the right of it. Strictly speaking, you do not need to draw the circle at all, merely the central dividing line.

The rune dice are cast directly over this vertical line so that they have an equal chance of coming to rest on either side. A die that lands on the line itself should be regarded as belonging to the left or right, depending on where the major portion of the die rests. If a die is

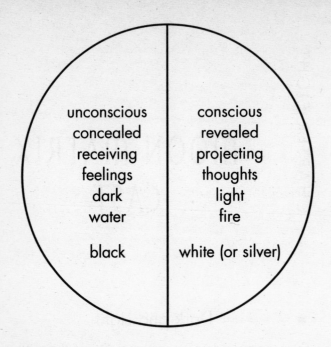

unconscious        conscious
concealed          revealed
receiving          projecting
feelings           thoughts
dark               light
water              fire

black              white (or silver)

**FIGURE 8.1.** The Moon Matrix.

so exactly centered on the line that you cannot clearly
determine whether it belongs to the left or right, consider it to occupy the line itself.

All the dualities associated with the Moon are
expressed in this matrix. The left side pertains to secret
and occult matters, the emotions, the unconscious
mind, dreams, hidden desires and suppressed
thoughts, illusions, fantasies, deceptions, black magic,
decay, death, the past, water, and in general everything
linked in myth and folklore to the dark. The right side
stands for matters of an overt or material kind, revelations, truth, reason, intellect, inspiration, growth, life,
the future, white magic, the conscious mind, fire, and
in general everything linked to the light.

The division of reality into two opposite sides makes this matrix ideal in questions that involve love, friendship, or close relations between the querent and another person. Such relationships include love affairs, marriages, business partnerships, friendships, sibling rivalries, enemies, or contestants in legal suits. In these cases, the querent will always see him or her self as the white half of the circle, which is the conscious half. The other member of the dual relationship will be placed by the querent in the dark, unknown, mysterious half of reality. For this reason, the runes that fall on the white half of the circle belong to the querent, while the runes that land on the black half belong to the other person.

The Moon Matrix may also be employed with good results in questions that concern the interaction or conflict between two groups. An organized body of humanity takes on its own collective soul and over time develops a kind of group consciousness. This expresses itself in the attitudes, rhetoric, and actions of its members. We see this in business organizations, religions, fraternities, schools and universities, social clubs, military and police organizations, political parties, elitist ideologies, social reform movements, intellectual movements, self-defined minorities, cultural, class, and age divisions.

We could use the duality of the Moon Matrix to probe relations between the Republican and Democratic parties, Macintosh and IBM, university faculty members and the student body, management and labor, blacks and whites, young and old, men and women, rich and poor, Catholics and Protestants, or any other clearly demarcated duality in our culture. When the duality is widely recognized, explicitly defined, and energized with social tension, it lends itself to a more fruitful analysis.

The Moon Matrix should mainly be confined to questions that involve relations between two social, professional, or political organizations that each have their own collective identity; a querent and another human being; or two opposed aspects of a querent's own nature. This is an excellent pattern matrix to resolve simple conflicts that may arise in a querent's personal life, and also to reveal conflicting elements in a querent's personality. Many of us find ourselves at war with parts of our own natures from time to time. The Moon Matrix serves to expose and contrast the good and bad qualities of an individual.

It is best to employ this pattern matrix, which concerns duality, with questions that can be answered on a basic level with a simple yes or no. The runes and their relative positions will provide more details that will explain this basic response. (As a general matter in divination by rune dice, questions should be kept simple and direct regardless of which pattern matrix is used—the more direct the question, the more explicit the answer given by the runes.)

## Moon Matrix, Sample Cast

A business woman in her late thirties wants to know whether her husband of two years is being unfaithful to her.

He is six years younger than she, works as a clerk in a large insurance firm, and earns only half what his wife earns through her book-selling business. When they first met, he was attempting to earn a living as a professional writer, but this ambition was put on hold indefinitely. His first novel is still unfinished. For the last five or six months he has grown increasingly distant, and has begun to adopt excuses for escaping from his wife's company, particularly her social activities.

When the rune dice were cast on the Moon Matrix
pattern, they formed the arrangement shown in Figure
8.2, below.

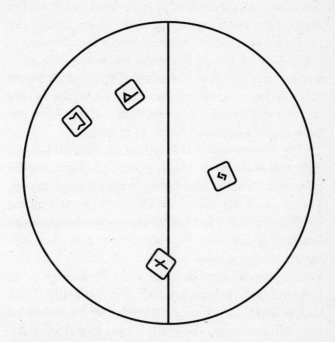

**FIGURE 8.2.** The fall of the dice in the Moon Matrix sample cast.

Three of the runes came to rest on the left side of
the matrix, and one on the right. The rune on the right
half of the circle, Jera (Ger) stands for the querent's role
or participation in the matter of the question. It means
harvest season or year, and by extension the end of a
cycle, revolution of fortune, and change. It is the turning wheel of time that never allows things to stay as
they were. Another aspect of this rune is the reaping of
what has been sown, the fulfillment of karma.

Touching the median line, but more in the dark half of the circle, lies Nauthiz (Nyd). In the context of the querent's question it probably signifies the unfulfilled and unexpressed yearnings of her husband. Because it lies closest to the diviner, it is the root of the matter under question. If we look further into the distance of the future, we perceive that these needs take the form of Perth (Peordh), which stands for sensual delights, games, and gambling, and Wunjo (Wyn), which means glory or joy. Since these two runes lie higher on the matrix than Nauthiz, it is probable that they have not been realized, certainly not to a full extent.

The interpretation is keyed by the rune Jera in the right half of the circle. This is a clear indication that the querent's domestic situation is in for a radical change. The cause of that transformation is suggested by the three runes in the left half of the circle. The querent's husband is unhappy with his present condition and feels unfulfilled. His fantasies and dreams take two forms: love affairs that involve a certain amount of risk; and personal success and glory, probably in the field of literature if we may be guided by his ambitions before his marriage. The Nauthiz rune suggests that the husband believes—rightly or wrongly—that he has been carrying a burden and suffering unfairly at the hand of fate.

My advice to the querent, based on this cast, would be to confront her husband and ask him directly what his feelings are about the marriage. This may precipitate a scene leading to the break-up of the union, but there is nothing to be gained by allowing the husband's resentment and unexpressed yearnings for love and glory to fester. He will only continue to grow more resentful and distant. It is possible that the two may come to some understanding if they talk matters out.

# TRINE MATRIX CAST

## ■——— Father-Mother-Child

The Trine Matrix pattern resembles the peace symbol from the 1960s. A large circle is divided into three wedges, one of which is centered at the bottom of the circle (Figure 9.1, page 112). If you paint a permanent Trine Matrix, color the bottom section of the circle yellow, the right section red, and the left section blue. As always, the outline itself should be black.

Conceive the circle as infinitely large. If one of the dice happens to roll outside it during a cast, in your mind extend the three lines that radiate from its center until you are able to determine on which section of the expanded circle the rogue die rests. The circle itself is not really needed to define this matrix, but is used merely to provide a more attractive shape to the pattern. If you cast the dice on the ground, or mark this matrix on some other rough surface, all you really require are the three lines that radiate outward at 120-degree intervals from a central point.

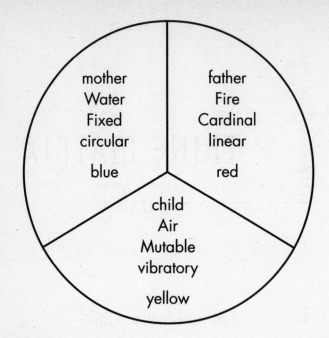

**FIGURE 9.1.** The Trine Matrix.

The most obvious physical model for the division of reality into three parts is the family unit, composed of father, mother, and child. It is expressed on a higher spiritual level in the divine trinities of many cultures, such as the Osiris-Isis-Horus family unit of ancient Egypt. Symbolically speaking, the two sexes are combined in the child, who is considered to be androgynous before puberty, when one or the other sex distinguishes itself. Sometimes the child is represented by twins in mythology. These may be male and female or good and evil.

To express the child as twins acknowledges the fundamental duality inherent in undeveloped life. The child partakes equally from its mother and father; therefore all dualities exist within the child in a potential state, awaiting manifestation. Since the child is both one as an androgynous product of duality, yet at the same time two as potentially male or female in its development, the family embodies the relationship between the numbers three and four that is central to the letters of the fourfold name of God, Tetragrammaton (IHVH). This most potent of all magical names is composed of both three letters, yet at the same time four letters, depending on whether the letters are considered by quality or quantity.

In Tetragrammaton, the first Hebrew letter (I) stands for the father principle. The second letter (the first H) stands for the mother principle. The third letter (V) by itself stands for the androgynous child, but when the child principle is differentiated into male and female, the two last letters taken together stand for a masculine child (V) and a feminine child (second H).

The division of reality into three parts also finds expression in the three dimensions of physical space (length, breadth, height). As pointed out earlier, these three spatial axes are incorporated into the design of the rune dice. Each of the three principles carries the seed of duality within itself, just as every person is formed of male and female parents. The dimension of length can be divided into right and left. The dimension of breadth can be divided into front and back. The dimension of height can be divided into up and down.

This duality of each dimension is expressed within the structure of Tetragrammaton by the permutation of the first three letters of the Name, IHV, which, as demonstrated in the explanation of the rune dice, may be divided into three pairs (IHV-IVH; HIV-HVI; VIH-VHI). The subtle complexities of Tetragrammaton are beyond the scope of the present work.[6] Here we are mainly concerned with the practical use of the rune dice for divination. I merely wish to stress that when we divide the circle into three, this is not a meaningless or arbitrary exercise, but allows us to apply the runes to one of the basic structural building blocks of reality.

The red section of the circle on the upper right relates to the father principle with all its associations of authority, strength, virility, leadership, aggression, dominance, violence, and law. It may be linked with the element Fire and with the Cardinal quality. Its motion is linear or expansive.

The blue section on the upper left part of the matrix is tied to the mother principle with all its symbolic and mythic associations of fertility, nurturance, reception, mysteries, secrets, beauty, illusions, enchantment, protection, and gentleness. It may also be linked with the element Water and with the Fixed quality. Its motion is circular or centered.

The yellow section at the bottom of the pattern matrix is associated with the child principle and its accompanying symbolic and mythic associations of innocence, hidden potential, growth, learning, evolution, changeability, capriciousness, playfulness, tricks, and magic. It may also be linked with the element Air and with the Mutable quality of astrology. Its motion is vibratory or changeable.

For seeking answers to questions that concern the family, the Trine Matrix is ideal. This includes extended families and social families such as clans, tribes, and fraternities as well as immediate families. The family does not need to be intact or bound by blood ties for it to be investigated with this matrix. For example, if the father happens to be dead, the runes that fall on the part of the father (red section) will apply to some father figure. This may be a relative, a friend, or even a woman who has assumed the role of authority figure within the family. Similarly, a child who has been adopted will still fill the role of child (yellow section)

in the matrix, even though he or she is not tied geneti-
cally to the father and mother figures.

## Trine Matrix, Sample Cast

A woman wants to know what she will inherit upon
the death of her stepmother, who is in failing health in
a nursing home.

The woman is forty-three years old, recently
divorced, with two children. Eleven years ago she had
an argument with her father and her sister about her
father's second marriage and stopped visiting her
father's house. When he died two years later, she did
not attend his funeral. She and her sister never speak or
visit each other. Her father left all of his estate to his
second wife. Over the last year the querent has been
visiting her stepmother in the nursing home and taking
her small gifts.

When cast upon the Trine Matrix, the runes fell in
the pattern shown in Figure 9.2 on page 116.

The nearest rune is Thurisaz (Thorn), which literally
translates as *devil*, and on a symbolic level indicates
malice, hatred, and evil. Since it lies within the yellow
section of the matrix, it stands for the querent in the
context of the question. It suggests that the querent's
feelings toward her stepmother have not been materi-
ally changed. She continues to resent and wish ill upon
the older woman.

The remaining three runes are clustered together in
the blue section of the matrix, and therefore pertain to
the mother figure in the querent's life, who in the context of the question is almost certainly the stepmother. The nearest rune, Hagalaz (Haegl) is the rune
that literally means *hail*. On a more general level it
stands for violence, rage, and destruction. The next

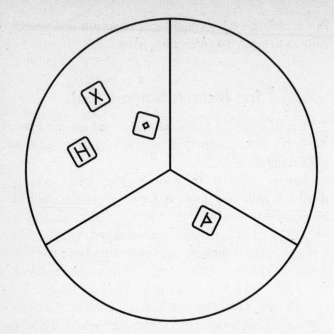

**FIGURE 9.2.** The fall of the dice in the Trine Matrix sample cast.

rune in distance from the diviner is Inguz (Ing), which indicates the family hearth and home. The final rune, Gebo (Gyfu) means a gift.

Notice that the three runes in the section devoted to the mother principle of the trinity are arranged in an almost equilateral triangle. This shows that they must all be considered together as a unit. It also suggests a favorable outcome for the querent. The line of the triangle formed by the runes Hagalaz and Inguz may be regarded as its base since the remaining fourth rune is opposite this line. This outside rune, Thurisaz, provides the basis for interpreting the triangle. In the context of the question Thurisaz suggests greed and malice.

Opposite to Thurisaz across the baseline of the triangle is Gebo, the rune signifying a gift. Gebo occupies the apex of the triangle, and in this position stands for the subject of the querent's interest, the inheritance money. The two runes on the baseline of the triangle indicate the process of uniting the base rune with the apex rune. Hagalaz (destruction) and Inguz (home) very clearly show that in her pursuit of her inheritance the querent will destroy her family.

There is a second more elongated triangle in this cast formed from the runes Thurisaz, Hagalaz, and Inguz. When we consider this as a unit, we find malice, rage, and the family. Inguz also signifies the father, suggesting that the root of the querent's hatred of her stepmother is a suppressed anger at her father for marrying a second time. The foundation of this triangle is the fourth rune, Gebo, the inheritance, and its apex is Thurisaz, greed and spiteful feelings. Because this triangle is more distorted, it has less impact on the matter of the question than the other triangle.

My interpretation of this cast is that the querent will indeed inherit from her stepmother, but that her stepmother will divide her estate in such a way that there will be constant strife and bickering between the members of the family, specifically between the querent and her sister. The triangle strongly suggests a favorable outcome for the querent with regard to the question, but this does not mean that the outcome will be happy. Between the querent and her prize lies family discord and conflict. A long legal battle may ensue after the death of her stepmother. There will probably be a delay before she receives the inheritance money, as indicated by the distance between her rune (Thurisaz) and the rune of the money (Gebo). Family strife stands in her path.

## CHAPTER TEN

# EARTH MATRIX CAST

## ■——— The Four Quarters

The Earth Matrix is a large circle divided through the center by a cross into four equal quarters (Figure 10.1, page 120). This pattern is used to answer questions of a material nature. It is reliable in questions that have to do with money, property, tangible assets and possessions, buildings and construction, collections such as stamps and coins, business ventures, investments, and physical health.

Like the square and the cube, the cross is a symbol of matter. The large circle of the matrix marks the outer limit of the physical universe. It should be conceptualized as infinitely large. Therefore if a die happens to roll out of the circle during a cast, merely extend the crossed lines at the center of the matrix in your own mind until you can determine which of the four quadrants the errant die rests upon. In fact, all you really need for this cast is the cross in the center of the matrix.

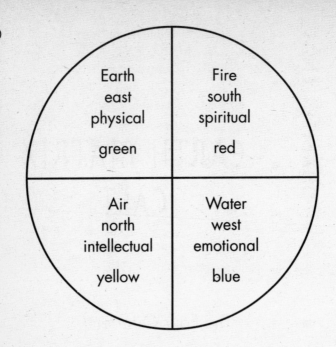

**FIGURE 10.1.** The Earth Matrix.

The four quarters of the circle are linked with the four directions, the four occult elements, and the four levels of the microcosm. The correspondences given here appear in my book *New Millennium Magick* (Llewellyn Publications: St. Paul, MN, 1996; originally titled *The New Magus*).

The quarter of the matrix on the upper right is linked with the direction south, the element Fire, and the level of spirit in the microcosm. If a permanent Earth Matrix is painted, this quarter should be bright red.

The lower right quarter is associated with the west, the element Water, and the level of emotion in the microcosm. If painted, this quarter of the matrix should be colored bright blue.

The lower left quarter of the matrix is located in the direction of the north, and takes the element Air, and the intellectual level of the microcosm. It should be colored bright yellow.

The upper left quarter of the matrix is linked to the east, the element Earth, and the level of physical matter in the microcosm. If painted on a permanent matrix, it should be colored bright green.

You may prefer to lay out the Earth Matrix using the popular Golden Dawn system of correspondences, which is more widely known and accepted. Under the Golden Dawn system, the upper left quarter of the circle belongs to the east, the element Air, the color yellow, and the level of intellect; the upper right quarter belongs to the west, the element Water, the color blue, and the level of emotion; the lower right quarter belongs to the south, the element Fire, the color red, and the level of spirit; the lower left quarter belongs to the north, the element Earth, the color black, and the level of the physical body.

It does not matter which system you choose, provided that you understand it and know that you are going to use it before you cast the dice. Never switch the system of occult correspondences in the middle of a divination.

Once you have picked a particular set of correspondences for the parts of a pattern matrix—any pattern matrix—your unconscious mind will accept that decision and work with it to provide you with an accurate interpretation of the cast. The more familiar you become with the correspondences of a particular matrix, the more rapidly and easily you will be able to read the runes. Understand that there is no absolute, right or wrong set of magical associations for the four quarters of the Earth. Individual occult correspondences take their meaning from their place in the system of correspondences as a whole. Beginners often do not realize this, and fasten onto one system of occult associations as the right one, while regarding all other systems as wrong. This attitude is narrow-minded and inhibits the learning process.

Since I am more familiar and comfortable with my own system, and believe that it makes better sense for a wide variety of reasons, I have used it for the Earth Matrix sample cast. The same basic principles of interpretation apply whether you decide to employ the Golden Dawn correspondences or those of *New Millennium Magick*.

## Earth Matrix, Sample Cast

A businessman is concerned about falling productivity in his plant, and wants to know if this is due to dissatisfaction among his work force.

The querent is fifty-two years old, divorced, with no children. His company, which he started from next to nothing eight years ago, assembles computer peripherals from stock parts. Lately he has been getting a higher than usual percentage of defective returns. The workers are paid an above average wage, but are often forced to work long hours and double shifts to meet the high demand for their products. The querent reports difficulties in finding enough skilled assembly workers, and recently has found it necessary to contract out some of his orders.

When the dice were cast upon the Earth Matrix, they fell in the pattern shown in Figure 10.2.

Two runes lie nearest to the diviner at almost the same distance, indicating a duel influence in the past, or in the background of the question that exists in the present. Hagalaz (Haegl), the rune of violent and

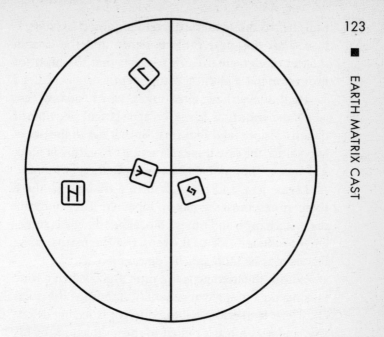

**FIGURE 10.2.** The fall of the dice in the Earth Matrix sample cast.

destructive winter storms, is in the lower left quarter, the quarter of Air and the north. This indicates intellectual unrest, because Air is the element of intellect. This dissatisfaction is expressing itself in the form of angry thoughts and inflammatory words.

Jera (Ger) is in the lower right quarter of the matrix, linked to the west, which points to an emotional change of attitude. Jera means harvest season, the end of a cycle. The western quarter of the matrix is the quarter of elemental Water, which signifies emotions and affection. Attitudes are changing for the worse.

Between these two runes on the upper edge of the northern quarter lies Algiz (Eolh), the rune of protection or defense. In the context of the question it may indicate the desire of the querent to protect his reputation. That this rune projects partly into the eastern quarter of elemental Earth suggests that the need for protection has a physical component.

High above these three runes, which occupy very nearly the same time frame, is Laguz (Lagu), the rune of dreams, visions, and illusions. Since it lies in the upper left quarter, the east, these visions are of a earthy or physical nature. They probably concern products or money.

Laguz, Jera, and Hagalaz form a triangle, so these three runes must be taken together. They indicate dreams, change, and unrest. Since the triangle is somewhat to the left side of the center of the matrix, these factors may be more psychological than actual.

Within the triangle is the rune Algiz. When a rune falls inside a triangle, it generally stands for the querent. Here, it suggests that the querent is feeling defensive, and sees himself pulled in three directions by his labor problems, his need to make changes in his business practices, and his desire to achieve a higher productivity and profit.

My interpretation of this cast is that changes instituted by the querent have caused unrest and anger among the workers, who feel that their livelihood is being threatened. However, the production problems are more a worry in the mind of the querent than a reality. He is driving himself to an unrealistic level of expectation because he seeks to attain an impossibly high goal of perfection, both in himself and by extension in his company. He will never attain the level he seeks no matter what measures he takes. He should adjust his production expectations to a realistic level and allow tempers to cool. The well-shaped triangle suggests that everything will come out favorably for the querent in the long run.

# STAR MATRIX CAST

## The Five Elements

This is another matrix that relies on the occult elements, but this time the Quintessence or fifth element of Spirit is added to the lower four. The circle of creation is divided by a star of five lines that radiate out from its central point (Figure 11.1, page 126). As always, the circle should be conceived to be of infinite size, and the lines radiating from its center as of infinite length.

A different element is placed into each of the five sectors that result from this division. Spirit is linked with the top part of the matrix. This sector should be colored white if the matrix is painted. Moving in a clockwise direction from Spirit, Water goes in the next sector, which should be painted blue, followed by Fire (red), Earth (green), and Air (yellow). If you prefer, you may substitute black for green as the color of Earth (black is the Golden Dawn color).

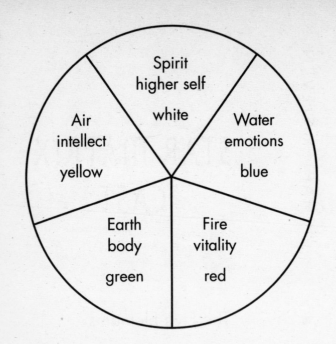

**FIGURE 11.1.** The Star Matrix.

This pattern matrix is ideal for questions that concern the balance of forces and qualities in the self, or within another person. The pentagram, or star of five points, is the symbol for the microcosm, or lesser world, just as the hexagram, or star of six points, is the symbol for the macrocosm, or greater world. Use this matrix when you wish to learn why an individual is acting a certain way, or holds a particular opinion. It is also excellent for accessing the innate strengths and weaknesses of a person.

The runes in this cast apply to the individual who is the subject of the question. The Star Matrix is the generic pattern for the microcosm in general. The runes cast upon it transform it into the pattern for the microcosm of a specific person. If you use if for self-divination, make sure that you always ask a very focused question each time you cast the dice. You should never ask the same question twice. Resist the urge to cast the runes a second time for a single question when you find that you do not like the response from the first cast. Always ask a clear, precise question before each cast, or else the response of the runes will be vague and generalized.

Spirit relates to the higher spiritual faculties and the Higher Self. The Higher Self is the part of human nature that is divine. This sector of the matrix reveals the religious beliefs and basic moral virtues of the subject of the cast. It can show the reason for a loss of faith or a sudden conversion to a different religion or credo. Runes in this sector reveal the spiritual maturity of an individual.

Water concerns love, affection, the emotions, dreams, and fantasies. This is the sector of wishes. It relates to the impulsive, irrational aspect of sexual attraction. Unconscious fears, desires, and suppressed thoughts are revealed by the runes that fall here. In general it is the part of the matrix that concerns the unconscious mind.

Fire is related to the vitality of the soul that animates and drives the body. It is the life force, and is usually said to reside in the blood. Sudden or violent impulses will be revealed by runes in this sector of the matrix. This is also the place of courage and will power. Strong runes here may indicate a dominating personality. This sector represents the reservoir of energy that causes a person to get up and accomplish a goal. Weak runes, or runes of an opposing element (for example Laguz, the water rune), would indicate weakness of will or lack of initiative.

Earth represents the physical part of a human being. Runes in this sector of the matrix reflect the state of health, physical strength, and endurance, and they foreshadow any future physical condition that may influence the outcome of the question. This sector also relates to physical sex, virility, and fertility. Unfavorable runes here may indicate sickness.

The sector of Air concerns reason, logic, cleverness, wit, inventiveness, intellectual capacity, the faculty of memory (but not memories themselves, which are watery), and the ability to use the written or spoken word to debate and persuade others. Favorable runes here may indicate a talent for politics, teaching, or the legal profession. Unfavorable runes may point to irrationality, mental dullness or slowness, and confused thinking.

## Star Matrix, Sample Cast

A woman wishes to know whether she is suited for a religious vocation.

She is thirty-seven years old, single, a devout Catholic, and has worked as a high school English teacher for the past sixteen years. Although she has had several serious boyfriends in the course of her life, for some reason all these relationships failed before marriage could be discussed; she believes that the fact that she is still single may be a sign from God that she has a calling to become a nun. She was an only child. Her father is dead, but her mother is still living. She sees her mother infrequently, usually not more than four times a year. It is her custom to travel in her car during the summer break. Her personal interests include architecture and opera.

When the dice were cast upon the Star Matrix, they fell in the pattern shown in Figure 11.2.

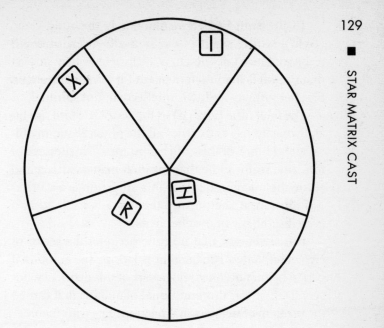

**FIGURE 11.2.** The fall of the dice in the Star Matrix sample cast.

The nearest rune to the diviner is Raido (Rad), literally a journey by horse. The horse was the only means of travel over land before the era of good roads. Today the same function is fulfilled by the car. Since the rune landed in the sector of elemental Earth, it concerns actual physical travel as opposed to a spiritual quest. It indicates that the querent has the wanderlust in her soul, and has traveled extensively in the past.

The next rune in distance and time is Hagalaz (Haegl), the rune of violent storms. Here in the sector of Fire, it shows that the querent has a violent and explosive temper. Her personality is aggressive, although she may suppress this tendency in her daily life. The need to constantly suppress her anger may cause frustration and dissatisfaction.

In the sector of elemental Air is the rune Gebo (Gyfu), which signifies either a gift given or a gift received. Since the querent is a teacher, we may suspect that the gift is her inherent talent for teaching. It shows that her primary ability is intellectual, not spiritual.

The final rune is Isa (Is) in the sector of Spirit. Isa literally means ice, and carries all the physical and mythical associations of this chilly substance. The message of this rune seems to be that spiritual matters attract and allure the querent, but that this attraction is a dangerous illusion. If she pursues them she is liable to find herself suddenly in over her head.

It is significant that no rune occupies the sector of elemental Water. The querent is lacking the emotional part of her nature. She is not aware of this deficiency, but very likely it was this emotional blandness that caused the breakup of her personal relationships with men.

My interpretation of this cast is that the querent is completely unsuited for the demanding vocation of a nun. Her interest in spiritual matters is mainly intellectual. Her present dissatisfaction for teaching stems from her suppressed hostility toward her work, hostility she must constantly keep in check. As an outlet she loses herself in travel during the summer. The spiritual world is for her only another vacation spot, a place to get away from her frustrations for a short while and experience something novel and intellectually interesting.

I would guess that if the querent did enter a religious order, before a year was over she would be just as frustrated and angry about her situation as she presently is about her teaching job. The best course for her would be to seek some employment where her intellectual gifts are stimulated and challenged, but where she is not called upon to use emotional skills that she simply does not possess.

CHAPTER TWELVE

# TIME MATRIX CAST

■————— The Hourglass of Time

The Time Matrix pattern is based on the figure of an hourglass set inside a large circle. The shape of the hourglass is simplified into two diagonal lines that cross at the center of the circle, and divide the circle into four zones (Figure 12.1, page 132).

The zone at the top of the matrix represents the future. The opposite zone at the bottom represents the past. The present moment is signified by the point where these two triangular sectors intersect at the middle of the circle. Think of this as an hourglass in which the sand falls from the upper zone through the middle point down to the bottom zone. The larger area on the left side of the matrix stands for hidden or unknown matters. The area on the right side stands for matters that are visible and known. The left zone also signifies the unconscious, and the right zone the conscious mind.

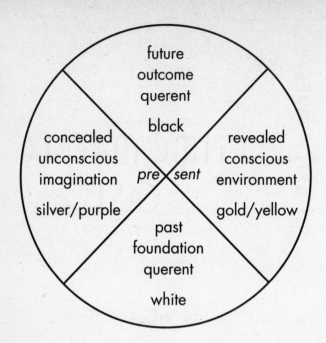

**FIGURE 12.1.** The Time Matrix.

As always, conceive of the circle as infinitely large. If one of the dice roles out of its boundary during a cast, extend the diagonal lines in your mind until the die lies within one of the four zones—it is not necessary to repeat the cast unless one or more of the dice rolls completely off the table. In fact, all you really need for the Time Matrix is two diagonal crossing lines. This makes it very easy to draw on the ground, the floor, or any convenient surface.

If you decide to make a formal Time Matrix pattern for regular use, color the zone of the future black (because the future is hidden), the zone of the past white (because it is known), the zone of the concealed either purple or metallic silver (colors of the Moon) and the zone of the revealed either yellow or metallic gold (colors of the Sun). The color combination white, black, silver, and gold is visually striking.

This matrix is useful when investigating the sequence and chronology of the events that lie behind the subject of the divination, because it allows us to quantify the times of significant actions relative to each other and to the present moment. We can determine whether something has already taken place or will happen in the future. We can judge how far apart in time events will occur, and whether or not they will be known to the querent. We can investigate how far into the past the foundation of the matter lies.

The Time Matrix is excellent when the querent is wondering if a certain thing is going to happen, and if so, when it is going to happen. This includes questions such as: "When will I win the lottery?" "Am I going to have a baby?" "Am I going to get married, and if so, when?" "Will my friend ever learn that I was unfaithful to her?" "Does my boss know that I've been stealing supplies from the office?" "Will I get a promotion?" "How long will my sickness last?" and so on.

It is not possible to measure these events in hours and days, but we can determine if something has already happened yet remains hidden, if it will happen very soon, or if it will not take place until the distant future. Sometimes it is possible to judge the scale of the timeline by the nature of the question. A question that covers a period of years or an entire lifetime has a much longer timeline that one that concerns events that are all in the relatively near future. For example, if the querent wants to know whether or not he or she will get a job for which the querent has submitted an application, we can assume that this will resolve itself before too many weeks one way or the other, so the timeline is relatively brief. Within this timeline we can determine from the runes whether the resolution will be immediate or delayed, and whether it will be favorable or unfavorable.

Runes that fall in the zone of the past can reveal underlying factors that may be influencing the matter of the question, yet remain completely hidden from the awareness of the querent. Sometimes the querent may be aware of these incidents in the past but have no idea that they are of any importance in the present question.

In general, runes that fall on the left half of the matrix indicate hidden factors or factors in the unconscious mind. Runes falling on the right half of the circle point to things that are well known or of a material nature. Runes in the lower half of the matrix point to past events or factors that are still influencing the question. Runes in the upper half or the matrix stand for things that have yet to come to pass. Runes falling within the hourglass shape of the timeline generally represent the querent. Runes falling outside the hourglass represent external factors acting upon the querent.

## Time Matrix, Sample Cast

A woman wants to know if she will receive a promotion, and if so, when.

She is in her early thirties, unmarried, and works as a bank clerk. A while ago she heard a rumor that she would be promoted to head teller, a position that carries a pay raise with it. However, three months have gone by with no sign that the promotion was anything more than a pipe dream. She has been considering moving away from the city in which she presently lives and works, but will put off plans for the move if the promotion is certain.

When cast upon the Time Matrix, the runes fell in the pattern shown in Figure 12.2.

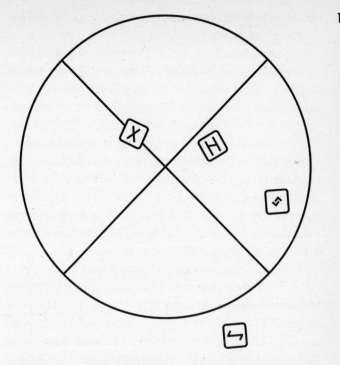

**FIGURE 12.2.** The fall of the dice in the Time Matrix sample cast.

The rune nearest to the diviner is Eihwaz (Eoh), which literally means *yew*, the tough, resilient wood used in war bows that is associated with the Underworld and the occult. It has fallen completely outside the circle of the matrix, but by mentally enlarging the circle and extending the crossed diagonal lines, we can see that it is within the zone of the past. It represents some factor in the subject of the divination that lies deep in the past of the querent's life, probably a defining influence on her character. It may signify the death of a role model that caused her to focus her goals in life, or it may merely indicate the querent's essential strength of character, which has allowed her to reach her present position.

The next rune is Jera (Ger), the rune of the end of a cycle and change. Because it is far to the right side of the zone of the conscious mind, this change will be of an outward, obvious kind. It is slightly below the center of the hourglass, showing that it has already occurred, or at least had its beginning in the near past.

Above it in the same zone of the manifest, the rune Hagalaz (Haegl) shows that there will soon be anger and violence of some kind in the physical environment of the querent. It is important to note that this rune does not lie within the hourglass itself, and therefore does not pertain directly to the querent.

The final rune is Gebo (Gyfu), signifying either a gift or a sacrifice. In the context of the question it probably stands for the promotion. This rune lies halfway in the zone of the querent's actual future, and halfway in the zone of the unconscious or concealed. A probable interpretation is that the promotion is not so valuable in the life of the querent as she believes. She may have been building up its benefits in her imagination.

The two runes Gebo and Hagalaz are located on the matrix at approximately the same distance from the diviner, indicating that these runes stand for events that will occur together or almost together in time. These two runes form a more or less straight line with Jera, tying the three together in a chain of causality. The change, which has its genesis in the near past, results in anger and disruption in the near future, which leads almost immediately to a gift or a sacrifice.

This is a difficult cast to interpret because there is nothing in the information supplied by the querent that explains the meaning of the rune Eihwaz, buried so deep in her past. It is probably some life-transforming event, which may have been the death of a loved one, that gave her a firm purpose and toughened her will.

The three remaining runes clearly have a direct bearing on the question. Since the querent learned of her possible promotion through a rumor three months ago, and the Jera rune, signifying change, is approximately as far below the present moment, indicated by the intersection of the diagonals, as the Gebo and Hagalaz runes are above it, the promotion will likely occur three months in the future. It will generate unrest in the querent's environment, but not in the querent herself. It may be speculated that one of the querent's coworkers is equally eager to obtain the job of head teller, and will be very disappointed when passed over, possibly to the point of committing some act of vandalism or destruction.

The querent probably will not find her new job as satisfying as she now believes. It will entail sacrifices on her part, and may in the end become as much a burden as a blessing. In a year or two the querent may end up moving from the city in which she presently lives, just as she plans to do if she does not get the promotion. My advice to her: proceed as though she is going to get the job of head teller, but do not expect it to change her life in wonderful ways or she will be disappointed.

# PLANET MATRIX CAST

## ■———— The Seven Spheres

The Planet Matrix relies on the symbols of the seven traditional planets of ancient astrology. It is formed out of a spiral that winds inward in a clockwise direction in three and a half turns. The spiral is divided down the middle by a vertical line. Each closed section of the spiral is linked with one of the planets. Beginning from the planet that is the slowest and farthest away and progressing to the planet that is nearest and quickest in motion, these are Saturn ($\hbar$), Jupiter ($\mathrm{2\!\!+}$), Mars ($\mathrm{O'}$), the Sun ($\odot$), Venus ($\mathbb{Q}$), Mercury ($\mathbb{Q}$), and the Moon ($\mathbb{D}$). (See Figure 13.1, page 140.)

While the Sun and the Moon are not planets, you should understand that we are not dealing with the actual physical bodies that circle the Sun through space, but with occult symbols of great antiquity and complexity. The Sun and Moon were grouped with the five planets that are easily visible to the naked eye

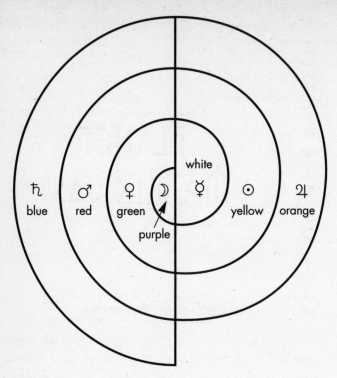

**FIGURE 13.1.** The Planet Matrix.

because they appear to move against the seemingly fixed background of the more distant stars. Together they make up the seven wandering bodies of the heavens, which were considered to differ from comets and meteors because their motions were cyclic and predictable, whereas meteors and comets were thought to be extraordinary, unpredictable events. (Some comets are predictable, but the ancient astronomers did not know this.)

The ancients regarded the seven planets as gods, and placed them in successive concentric transparent spheres that turned one inside the other at different velocities. They ordered these spheres by their apparent rates of motion, reasoning that the slowest planet, Saturn, must be the farthest away from the Earth, which was always placed at the center of the universe. This arrangement of the planets is usually called Ptolemaic, named after one of its main exponents, the Greek astronomer Claudius Ptolemaeus, who lived in the second century.

The set of symbolic meanings associated with the seven planets of traditional astrology is incredibly rich and may be applied to a wide variety of life situations. It has been used in connection with divination by astrologers since the age of the ancient Egyptians and Babylonians. When the planets are used as a pattern matrix in rune divination, this wealth of meaning becomes available as an aid in interpreting the runes.

The best use for the Planet Matrix is full life readings. The planets are closely tied to the seven ages or phases of human life, which are most familiar from the description given by Shakespeare in his comedy *As You Like It*.[7] There is disagreement among ancient writers over the spans of the ages, but general concord in ordering them upon the planetary spheres. I will give here the terms of the ages supplied by Ptolemy in his astrological work *Tetrabiblos*.[8]

Ptolemy says that the Moon relates to infancy (birth to four years), Mercury to childhood (five to fourteen years), Venus to youth (fifteen to twenty-two years), the Sun to the prime of life (twenty-three to forty-one years), Mars to adulthood (forty-two to fifty-six years), Jupiter to maturity, the time of greatest wisdom (fifty-seven to sixty-eight years), and Saturn to the frailty and decline of the faculties of old age (sixty-nine years to death).

The spiral of the matrix should not be conceived to stop at the zone of Saturn, but to continue winding ever outward just as the starry universe extends endlessly away on all sides of the Earth. After the sphere of Saturn in the Ptolemaic system comes the sphere of the fixed stars or the zodiac. For the purposes of rune divination, any die that rolls outside the boundary of the spiral should be understood to lie in the zone of the zodiac. It should be associated with the afterlife.

Those who possess a good knowledge of astrology may wish to extend the spiral to include zones for the outer planets, Uranus, Neptune, and Pluto. This can easily be accomplished by adding one and a half additional turns to the spiral. Personally, I have very little use for the outer planets, either in divination or in magic. While astrology as an art of divination is many thousands of years old, all three of the outer planets have only been known to exist since the discovery of Pluto in 1930. Perhaps someday in the future they will be successfully incorporated into astrology. At present they are artificially tacked onto the tail end of the elegant and complete ancient system, and serve no necessary function in that system.

The ancient colors of the planets may be used to color the zones of the matrix. The Moon is silver or white, Mercury is red-orange, Venus is emerald green, the Sun is gold or lemon yellow, Mars is ruby red, Jupiter is sky blue, and Saturn is black. The colors of the planets that I prefer to use in my own personal work with this matrix are taken from my *New Millennium Magick* system.[9] For those who may be interested in working with this set of colors, they are: Moon (purple), Mercury (white), Venus (green), Sun (yellow), Mars (red), Jupiter (orange), Saturn (dark blue). It is not a matter of great importance which set of colors are used, since in rune divination the colors of the matrices are purely decorative.

When you draw the spiral of the Planet Matrix, it is

easier if you trace the line from the center outward. This way you will not find yourself cramped for space, as can happen if you draw the spiral from the outside inward. Make the spaces between the loops of the spiral wide enough so that they will easily hold the dice— about three inches between the successive revolutions of the spiral allows ample space for the dice to fall. A rune is considered to occupy the planetary zone that contains the largest part of its die. If the die lands exactly on top of a line, with equal amounts in two adjacent zones, it should be read as though it belongs to both zones equally.

In addition to the seven phases of human life, the traditional planets also carry complex meanings that are helpful in reading the runes. You should study a basic textbook on astrology for a deeper understanding of these life principles.

Moon—Duality, the unconscious, cycles, biorhythms, habits, dreams, mental problems, memories, instincts, the past, pregnancy, the mother figure, the home, growth and decay, the emotions, reactions.

Mercury—Communication, intelligence, curiosity, analysis, lack of emotion, quickness, cleverness, eloquence, messages, the written word, legal matters, magic, deception, mischievous, the child figure, a teacher or guide.

Venus—Love, understanding, sympathy, deep feelings, passivity, subjective experiences, a serene nature, reception, cooperation, artistry, an aesthetic sensibility, the creative impulse, a need for affection, good fortune, the acquisition of money or possessions, the figure of the lover.

Sun—Wholeness of the personality, the center of life, spirit, consciousness, harmonious balance, completeness, integration, the father figure, constancy, the self in relation to the larger universe, and a sense of identity.

Mars—Activity, self-assertion, enterprise, will-power, courage, impulsiveness, sexual passions, virility, dominance, combativeness, risk-taking, impatience, cruelty, conflict, the figure of the warrior.

Jupiter—Maturity, confidence, poise, understanding, success, authority, judgment, joviality, physical and mental expansion, attainment, well-being, robust health, a protector, the figure of the ruler.

Saturn—Discipline, limitation, restriction, penetration, occult teachings, time, rigidity, melancholy, seriousness, study, practical considerations, self-denial, science, religion, the figure of the teacher.

## Planet Matrix, Sample Cast

A young man wants to know if he should become a writer. He is twenty-three years old, single, presently without a girlfriend, lives at home with his parents, and has just completed a university arts degree with a major in English literature. He has decided to take a year off before deciding whether to continue with his education or look for a job, and is playing with the notion of using the time to try to establish himself as a freelance fiction writer. While in college he had two short stories and several poems published in various university magazines, all of them without payment, and in his final year at college he won a literary competition at his own university. However, he confesses that the rejection slips he has received for his fiction when he has sent his stories to professional magazines caused him severe anxiety and depression. He wonders whether he has what it takes to make a career of writing.

When the rune dice were cast on the Planet Matrix, the following pattern appeared (Figure 13.2).

The rune nearest the diviner is Perth (Peordh), which stands for sensual indulgence and pleasure. Since it has fallen into the zone of the Sun, and the time frame occupied by the Sun in the seven ages of

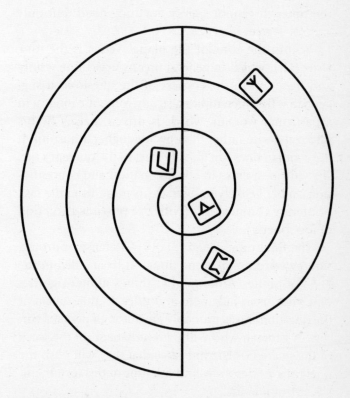

**FIGURE 13.2.** The fall of the dice in the Planet Matrix sample cast.

human existence (twenty-three to forty-one years) includes the age of the querent (twenty-three), we may safely say that this rune stands for the essential nature of the querent in relation to the question. It is a love of physical and mental ease, sloth, luxury, and pleasure.

The next rune, Thurisaz (Thorn), occupies the zone of Mercury, which stands for the intellectual capabilities of the querent. In the present context Thurisaz signifies prejudice, narrow-mindedness, dullness, lack of originality, deceit, and quite possibly plagiarism. Thurisaz is a very bad rune. Indeed, it is the worst of all the runes. It cannot signify anything good, but only various degrees of evil.

Within the zone of the planet Venus is the rune Uruz (Ur), which in general means masculine virility and freedom. In the context of the question, it suggests that the querent has a strong romantic interest in a particular woman, which is driven mainly by his physical desire rather than by any higher attraction. If this woman does not already exist in the querent's life, she will soon enter it. His fascination and concentration on her is likely to distract his mind from the task of literary composition (with the possible exception of love poetry).

The final rune is Algiz (Eolh)—defense or protection by warding off some threat. It has landed in the zone of Jupiter. Among other things Jupiter signifies one who sits in judgment and rules. In the context of the question this is probably an editor, or perhaps editors in general, who will pass judgment on the work of the querent. Algiz indicates that they will push the querent's stories away and attempt to distance themselves from them.

Three runes, Perth, Thurisaz, and Uruz, form a roughly straight line, and so should be interpreted as a connected succession of events. They stand for a pleasure-loving nature, a mean and limited intellectual capacity, and a disinclination to endure discipline.

Taken as a whole, it would not be possible to imagine a more negative response from the runes to the querent's question. They say he is utterly unsuited to be a writer, which requires a willingness to suffer hardship and rejection, an innate talent for original thought, and a capacity for self-discipline. My interpretation is that if the querent attempts to write, he will quickly become tired of the concentrated effort or will be distracted from his purpose by his new love interest, or both. Any stories or essays he does submit to magazines will be rejected. There is also a suggestion from Thurisaz in Mercury that he might try to avoid the labor of creating his own stories by stealing those of other writers. Almost any occupation would suit this young man better than freelance writing.

## CHAPTER FOURTEEN

# ZODIAC MATRIX CAST

## The Zodiac Signs and Their Houses

The Zodiac Matrix is formed from a large circle that has been divided through its center by six lines, resulting in twelve wedge-shaped zones. Each zone occupies the space of an hour on the face of the clock, and is linked with one of the signs of the zodiac (Figure 14.1, page 150). The signs are arranged around the matrix counterclockwise, beginning on the left, in the order they usually appear in astrology: Aries (red), Taurus (red-purple), Gemini (purple), Cancer (blue-purple), Leo (blue), Virgo (blue-green), Libra (green), Scorpio (yellow-green), Sagittarius (yellow), Capricorn (yellow-orange), Aquarius (orange), Pisces (red-orange).

The set of colors applied to the zones of the matrix are those used in my *New Millennium Magick* system. If you prefer, you may wish to use the elemental colors for each sign of the zodiac. Aries ($\Upsilon$), Leo ($\Omega$), and

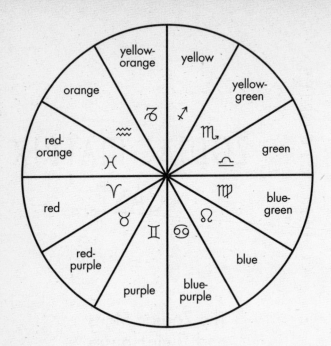

**FIGURE 14.1.** The Zodiac Matrix.

Sagittarius ($\nearrow$) are Fire signs, and therefore may be colored red; Cancer ($\odot$), Scorpio ($\mathrm{M}$), and Pisces ($\mathrm{H}$) are Water signs, and may be colored blue; Libra ($\triangle$), Aquarius ($\approx$), and Gemini ($\mathrm{II}$) are Air signs, and may be colored yellow; Capricorn ($\zeta$), Taurus ($\forall$), and Virgo ($\mathrm{M}$) are Earth signs, and may be colored green (or black).

A rune falling into the zone of a sign can be interpreted in two ways, depending on whether it is considered to be within the sign itself or the natural house of that sign. Zodiac signs and their natural houses are very closely related. For the sake of simplicity, the sign of each zone will be described in terms of the type of activity the runes that land in it will exhibit, and the corresponding house of that zone will be described in terms of the matters acted upon by runes landing in the zone. This dual interpretation for each zone of the way the runes act, and the matters they act upon, lends a great deal of flexibility in analyzing the meaning of casts on the Zodiac Matrix.

Each sign of the zodiac is associated with one of the four ancient elements (Fire, Water, Air, Earth) and one of the three astrological qualities (Cardinal, Mutable, Fixed). Their combination constitutes the underlying basis for the meaning of each sign.

You do not need to know anything about constructing an astrological chart or reading heavenly aspects to use the Zodiac Matrix cast. It is only necessary to have a basic understanding of what the signs and their corresponding houses mean. Below is a list of meanings for the signs and their houses. It will add depth to your reading of the runes on the Zodiac Matrix if you study more about the signs and houses on your own, using an introductory text on astrology as your guide. The better you know the signs, the clearer and more precise your reading of the runes will be.

Aries—(Fire-Cardinal); Active, energetic, self-assertive, impulsive, restless, impatient, courageous, risk-taking, leading, direct, insensitive, challenging, urgent, foolhardy.

First House— Physical characteristics of an individual, essential nature, self-centered interests, the querent.

Taurus—(Earth-Fixed); Self-restrained, passive, reliable, trustworthy, enduring, patient, productive, cautious, deliberate, practical, economic, insecure, tedious.

Second House—Possessions, money, things produced, personal security, creature comforts.

Gemini—(Air-Mutable); Adaptable, versatile, restless, curious, changeable, talkative, clever, inconsistent, fickle, communicative, mentally agile, self-expressive.

Third House—Communication, messages, letters, conversations, teaching or learning, lecturing, news reporting, writing, relations between brothers and sisters, or neighbors.

Cancer—(Water-Cardinal); Protective, tenaciously loyal, sympathetic, maternal, sentimental, intuitive, moody, self-reserved, mediumistic, emotional, defensive, sensitive to slights, self-pitying.

Fourth House—The mother, family, the home, owned land or buildings, the womb, the grave, mystical matters, the unconscious mind.

Leo—(Fire-Fixed); Prideful, enthusiastic, magnetic, generous, dignified, self-assured, self-controlled, authoritative, commanding, bold, creative, pompous, conceited, sensual.

Fifth House—The father, writers, actors, artists, pleasures, games, gambling, stock market speculations, risk-taking, racing, love-making and lovers.

Virgo—(Earth-Mutable); Critical, analytical, discriminating, efficient, perfection-seeking, reserved, shrewd, assimilative, fastidious, puritanical, inhibited.

Sixth House—Public service, health care, matters of hygiene, diet, inspectors, art critics, statisticians, chartered accountants, nursing, teaching, technical work.

Libra—(Air-Cardinal); Harmonious, compromising, cooperative, balanced, indecisive, charming, gentle, romantic, sentimental, flirtatious, tactful, vacillating.

**Seventh House**—Partners, a husband or wife, friends, close companions, a lover, relationships with other persons.

**Scorpio**—(Water-Fixed); Intense, penetrating, secretive, purposeful, subtle, mystical, intuitive, suspicious, vindictive, cruel, passionate.

**Eighth House**—Inheritances, legacies, sex, psychic abilities, jealousy, hate, revenge, death.

**Sagittarius**—(Fire-Mutable); Free-spirited, seeking, foresighted, aspiring, open-minded, idealistic, ambitious, adventurous, exploring, restless, high-strung, nervous.

**Ninth House**—Deep studies, philosophy, religion, distant travel, prophecy, publishing, horses, the law, dreams.

**Capricorn**—(Earth-Cardinal); Cautious, patient, persevering, resourceful, persistent, responsible, modest, serious, miserly, stern, selfish, emotionally cool.

**Tenth House**—Career, social status, one's place in the world, appointments, promotions, rank, title, type of work, responsibilities outside the home.

**Aquarius**—(Air-Fixed); Emotionally detached, freedom-loving, original, persuasive, independent, paradoxical, progressive, opinionated, perverse, eccentric, erratic, rebellious, inventive.

**Eleventh House**—Acquaintances, social groups, membership in organizations, political causes, social movements, hopes and wishes.

**Pisces**—(Water-Mutable); Emotionally unstable, sensitive, impressionable, impractical, dreamy, unfocused, imaginative, intuitive, compassionate, gullible, sub-missive, indecisive, mediumistic.

**Twelfth House**—Sacrifice, seclusion, hidden things, hospitals, prisons, mental institutions, religious orders, the sea, the unconscious, deception. Traditionally called "the house of one's own undoing."

You will notice that similar descriptive terms some-times appear under more than one sign. Signs that share basic elements also share similar modes of expression. By studying all the terms for each sign and weighing them together, you can form a collective understanding of that sign, and you will quickly see how it differs from all the rest.

In divining by rune dice, the meanings under the houses are more useful in a practical sense than the descriptive terms under the signs, because the houses reveal manifest conditions and physical things. The runes are by their nature very direct and explicit in their meanings. The signs are useful in analyzing human character, the houses are useful in analyzing human conditions. When brought together they give a very complete picture of the subject of the divination.

The Zodiac Matrix is best used to investigate all the effects of the matter under question in the life of the querent. Large matters with far-reaching consequences that touch on the home, the career, family, friends, life-goals, and the greater environment of the querent will yield the most fruitful results. Use this pattern when the question cannot be expressed in such a way that it is possible to answer it with a simple yes or no. Such questions include things such as: "Where am I going with my life?" "What does my lover really think about me?" "How can I improve my personality?" "Why does my father hate me?" "Why am I always getting sick?" "How can I advance my career?" and so on.

A truck driver wants to know why he never went to college. He is forty-two years old, and has been working in long-haul trucking for over twenty years. When he was a teenager he showed an advanced talent for mathematics, and the rest of his grades were always above average. His parents wanted him to get a university degree in business administration. They offered to pay his complete tuition and expenses. Instead of accepting, the querent left home and drifted from one part-time job to another for a year, until finally he was hired as a driver by a trucking company. He has held the same job ever since.

He is married, has two children, a house in a good neighborhood with no mortgage, and is completely happy, but he still wonders what made him decline to attend college, when he had been so enthusiastic about the prospect of getting a business degree.

When the rune dice were cast on the Zodiac Matrix, the result was the pattern shown in Figure 14.2 (see page 156).

The near rune, Gebo (Gyfu), lies in the zone of Gemini and the Third House. The rune itself signifies a gift or sacrifice, possibly both. In the context of the question, the gift involved is probably the inborn talent of the querent. Gemini indicates restlessness, curiosity, changeability, and fickleness, but also communication, self-expression, and the ability to talk. The Third House stands for conversation and communication. In general, the Third House is the relationship between the self and the environment.

The next rune in distance from the diviner is Jera (Ger). It lies directly on top of the dividing line between Virgo and Libra. Jera itself signifies the end of a cycle and change. Virgo indicates a critical, discriminating,

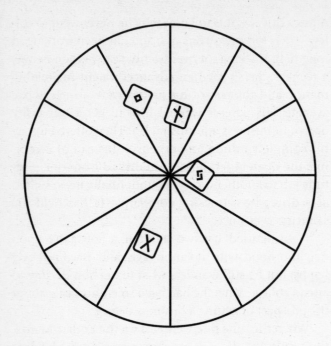

**FIGURE 14.2.** The fall of the dice in the Zodiac Matrix sample cast.

and analytical faculty, and its corresponding house stands for, among other things, statistics and accounting. Libra, on the other hand, is the faculty of romantic impulses, indecision, vacillation, and sentimentality. Its house indicates a partnership, friendship, or relationship with another person.

Because the rune of change has fallen directly between these two signs, it strongly suggests that the signs Virgo and Libra, along with their natural houses, represent the choice that faced the querent, whether he should be practical and study accounting and business, or instead indulge his romance for the open road. The Earthy, Fixed part of his nature, represented by Virgo, was in direct conflict with his Airy, Cardinal qualities, represented by Libra. His wanderlust may have been driven by a need to meet other individuals with whom he could share his thoughts and feelings on the personal level.

The third rune, Nauthiz (Nyd) stands for the endurance of suffering, or more simply, pain. It lies in the sign Sagittarius, which means idealism, restlessness, a love of adventure and exploration, a search for new experience. The corresponding Ninth House stands for long-distance travel and dreams, and also deep study or profound thoughts.

The final rune, Inguz, is the rune of the home and family. It lies within Capricorn, the sign of patient perseverance and resourcefulness, dedication to a practical purpose, the determined climb up the ladder of social success. Its house indicates career, the querent's place in the world.

Since the last two runes considered rest within the length of a die of each other, they must be examined together. The suffering or yearning of the Nauthiz rune on the sign Sagittarius, which is the sign of exploration and long-distance travel, is placed in direct contrast to the home and hearth, the rune Inguz, which in the context of the question probably also stands for the father, on the sign Capricorn, the sign of social advancement in the world and pursuit of career goals.

There are three dualities in this cast. One is the indecision that seethed within the querent over whether he should pursue his talent with numbers and pay attention to his sense of practical necessity and duty, or surrender to his romantic and irrational desire for communication and social contact with like-minded individuals. This is represented quite clearly by the rune of change, Jera, balanced between Virgo and Libra.

The second duality was between the querent's inner need to travel and find adventure on the open road, and his parents' wish that he should be practical and climb the social ladder to success. This is shown by Nauthiz on Sagittarius immediately opposite Inguz on Capricorn.

The third duality is expressed within the single rune Gebo, which means both *gift* and *voluntary sacrifice*, a gift received or a gift given. Implicit in the meaning of Gebo is the notion that to receive something of value you must give something of equal worth as payment. Mutable Gemini is the sign of the twins, and is inherently double. To acknowledge the gift of his talent for mathematics, the querent would have been forced to sacrifice his romantic dreams of venturing out into the wide world to interact with others he could relate to on the personal level. He had a second gift not perceived or acknowledged by his parents, a gift he longed with all his heart to express, and in the end did express—the gift for communicating with people.

Since the querent is settled and happy in his present life, it appears that he made the correct decision when he struck out on his own for travel and adventure, rather than deny his inner dream and resign himself to a lifetime of business administration. The temporary anguish of disappointing his parents was replaced by a contented life that allows him to do what he loves to do most—travel far and wide and experience new places and new faces.

CHAPTER FIFTEEN

# MULTIPLE-CAST DIVINATION

■─────── ## Limitations of Single-Cast Divination

Divining with a single cast of the dice, whether this is done on the blank surface of the Sky Matrix or upon one of the more complex patterns such as the Planet Matrix, is excellent for investigating most questions. It is quick, simple, and direct. When the question is also kept simple and may be answered in a preliminary way with a yes or a no, the result is a form of divination that has no match for clarity.

This clarity of meaning stems from the simplicity of the runes themselves. Each rune represents only one thing, which may be a physical object, a mythical being, a force of nature, or a human quality. The additional levels of meaning for each rune are directly derived from its essential basic meaning. However, these basic meanings are all archetypes, allowing a wealth of secondary symbolic significance to be added onto them as the need arises.

There is one serious limitation to divination by a single cast of the rune dice. Astute readers have probably already perceived it. Because each die holds six runes, and only one rune can land uppermost with each cast of that die, it is impossible for two runes on any single die to interact in a single cast. For example, Berkana and Fehu will never occur together in a single cast because they occupy the same die. This limits the number of possible combinations of the runes significantly. In fact, there are 1,296 combinations of runes possible in a single cast (6 x 6 x 6 x 6).

In many ways this limitation is useful. It simplifies the interpretation of the runes, and makes learning rune divination by single casts very easy, even for beginners who have never divined before. Any of the twenty-four runes can occur in any single cast, so there is no restriction on which runes appear, only on which combinations appear.

For those who wish to divine with the rune dice, but do not want to be restricted in the number of combinations of runes that appear, there is a simple solution—divination by multiple casts of the dice. When the dice are thrown two or more times in succession, and the runes of each cast recorded together on a piece of paper, the possible combinations are, for all practical purposes, unlimited.

## Futhark Matrix, Multiple Cast

This multiple-cast divination employs the framework of the elements and qualities of astrology as they are assigned to the rune pairs in the three aettir of the futhark (refer to the table of rune correspondences in chapter four). The runes are cast three times, then written in order on the grid of the Futhark Matrix, which has three rows and four columns. The runes of the first cast are placed on the bottom row of the pattern, the runes of the second cast on the middle row, and the runes of the third cast on the top row.

Runes are placed on the rows from left to right, the direction in which runes are most commonly read. The first rune in each row is the rune that falls nearest the diviner in the cast, the second rune in the row is the next farther away, and so on. The correct placement of the runes is clearly shown in Table 15.1 by numbers one to twelve.

| Cast | Time | Elements | | | | Qualities |
|------|------|------|-------|-----|-------|-----------|
| | | Fire | Water | Air | Earth | |
| 3rd | Future | 9 | 10 | 11 | 12 | Cardinal |
| 2nd | Present | 5 | 6 | 7 | 8 | Mutable |
| 1st | Past | 1 | 2 | 3 | 4 | Fixed |

**TABLE 15.1.** The correct placement of the runes in the Futhark Matrix, multiple cast.

The application of the elements and qualities to this matrix is an evolution of a simpler technique for divination by three casts of the dice given in my book *Rune Magic*.[10] In the earlier method the runes are arranged upon the same matrix of three rows and four columns, but the runes are related to the twelve houses of the zodiac in sequential order from one to twelve, the first rune in the cast to the First House, the second rune to the Second House, the third rune to the Third House, and so on. This older method works well and gives good readings, but I wanted to integrate this pattern of the runes more fully with the German futhark.

The Futhark Matrix reconciles the underlying structure of the zodiac to the structure of the futhark. Each sign and its natural house is based on the combination of one of the four elements (Fire, Water, Air, and Earth) and one of the three qualities (Cardinal, Mutable, Fixed). As I mentioned in chapter fourteen, the mingled element and quality of a sign is the true fundamental meaning of that sign. Everything else associated with the sign is either an extrapolation from its element-quality foundation, or has merely been tacked onto the sign and over the centuries has been accepted on the strength of its tradition of use.

By combining the element and quality, we get a sign and its corresponding natural house for each of the twelve runes in the cast. For example, rune number seven is associated by its position in the matrix with the element Air and the Mutable quality. The sign of Mutable Air is Gemini, and its natural house is the Third House. Similarly, the tenth rune is linked with the element Water and the Cardinal quality, so its zodiac sign is Cancer, the sign of Cardinal Water, and its house is the Fourth, which is the natural house of Cancer.

The bottom row of the matrix gives insight into the past, the middle row clarifies the present, and the top row reveals the future. The past is by its nature fixed and unalterable, so it receives the Fixed quality. The present is the time of decisions and choices, when your life can branch out in one direction or another depending on how you choose to act, so it receives the Mutable quality. The future extends like a quiver of arrows into the limitless unknown, each arrow a different potential timeline in your future that will only come into existence when you make the decision that creates it. Therefore, the future is associated with the Cardinal quality.

Runes that are next to each other on the matrix should be considered related in meaning. When they are adjacent on a column, the rune below acts earlier in time than the rune above, and influences the rune above it by its action. When adjacent runes are on a row, the rune to the left has a causal influence on the rune on the right, just as thought precedes and influences action. All of the runes influence other runes or are influenced by other runes, with the exception of the first rune, which influences its two adjacent runes but is not influenced itself, and the twelfth rune, which is influenced by its adjacent runes but influences nothing. The first rune is the beginning of the matter under question, the twelfth rune is its ending (insofar as anything can be said to begin or end in the limitless river of time).

The meanings for the elements and qualities have already been given in chapter four, and the meanings for the signs and houses of the zodiac have been provided in chapter fourteen. You should refer to these chapters when using the Futhark Matrix until you gain confidence that you know the elements, qualities, signs, and houses well enough to perform this cast on your own. You will also find these meanings listed in simplified form in the quick reference guide to reading the rune dice in the appendix.

## Futhark Matrix, Sample Cast

A man wishes to learn more about the background and true nature of a woman to whom he is about to propose marriage. His specific question: should he ask her to marry him?

He is forty-one years old, has never been married before, and is employed in an administrative position at a major university. He met his potential future bride on a cruise ship while on a sight-seeing tour of antiquities in the Mediterranean. She is twenty-nine years old, divorced with no children, and an amateur archaeologist. They soon learned that they shared common interests in science and literature, spent a great deal of time together, and continued to visit each other and communicate by telephone and e-mail after the tour concluded. However, he has never met the woman's family and confesses that he actually knows very little about her personal life, other than that she was born in the Midwest, is an only child, and that her father died some time ago.

When the runes were cast three times and recorded on the grid of the Futhark Matrix, the pattern shown in Figure 15.1 emerged.

The first rune is Mannaz (Man). This may indicate either the distinguishing human qualities of intelligence and free will, or may simply stand for a human being. It is conditioned by the element Fire and the Fixed quality, and therefore the sign Leo and the Fifth House of the zodiac. A Leo person is honorable, brave, and noble, but sometimes has the faults of vanity and a love of pleasure. The Fifth House stands for creativity and also for fatherhood. This rune is the beginning of the question. The element Fire places this rune on the microcosmic level of spirit. The interpretation is: a noble and forceful human spirit, perhaps arrogant and overbearing.

The second rune is Fehu (Feoh), literally *cattle*, which may stand for material possessions, wealth, or a subservient role in human relations. The watery element indicates instability, whereas the Fixed quality suggests intense and determined feelings. Fixed Water is

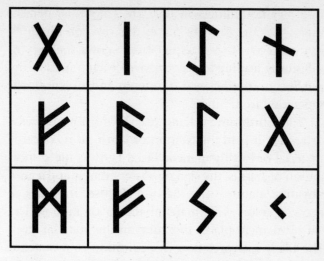

**FIGURE 15.1.** The rune pattern from the Futhark Matrix sample cast. The runes were cast three times and recorded on the grid.

the combination of Scorpio, the sign of passionate emotions, deep convictions, and strong sexual impulses. The natural house of Scorpio is the Eighth House, indicating that this rune pertains to a legacy of some kind, perhaps feelings or possessions gained from another person. The watery element places this rune on the emotional level. The interpretation is: feelings of inferiority give rise to strong but secret resentments.

The third rune is Sowelu (Sigel), literally a ray or lightning stroke that falls from the Sun, or perhaps a blazing meteor. By extension, it is the intervention of heaven in earthly affairs, which is often interpreted as a judgment. Because this rune rests upon the column of Air, it may signify a brilliant and penetrating intellect. Fixed Air is the combination of Aquarius, the sign of strong intellectual opinions that may be cherished to the point of fanaticism or lead to eccentric behavior. It

indicates faithfulness in love but emotional detach-
ment. The airy element places this rune on the intellectual level. The interpretation shows feelings of
inferiority leading to an excessive development of the
intellect in specific areas of interest and an emotional
separation from others.

The fourth rune is Kano (Cen), which means *torch*
or *beacon*. It is in the column of Earth, so it concerns
material or earthly matters. Fixed Earth is the combination of Taurus, the sign of possessiveness and a con-
servative nature. The Second House indicates a
preoccupation with material things or money. The
earthy element places this rune on the material level.
The likely interpretation is: dedication to a material
goal that involves the acquisition of possessions.

These four runes together present a picture of the
past or background that has influenced the present
nature of the woman the querent wishes to marry. We
can be fairly confident that the runes relate to the
woman and not to the querent because the main concern in the querent's mind is the true nature of his
future bride. The first rune, Mannaz, is probably the
woman's father, a proud, strong, and resourceful man
with high expectations of his daughter. Unable to live
up to her father's expectations, the woman developed a
feeling of inferiority and low self-esteem, as indicated
by the Fehu rune and the square of Scorpio. She
attempted to compensate for this by suppressing her
emotions and concentrating on her intellectual development. By nature she has a penetrating intellect
(Sowelu on Aquarius). This is directed in an intense
manner on a single goal or pursuit, probably her desire
to achieve some discovery of importance in her hobby
of archaeology (Kano on Taurus), which has to do with
the Earth. She would probably have made archaeology

her main profession, but her low sense of self-worth 167
prevented her from pursuing this goal in her early life.

The fifth rune is again Fehu, the rune of submission
and servitude, but also of valuable property. It rests in
the place of Mutable Fire, the sign of Sagittarius, indicating an intellectual and questing nature, exploration,
and long or frequent journeys. Fire gives this sign passion, but the Mutable quality makes this passion unstable and capricious. Sagittarius yearns to be free, and
may marry late in life. The Ninth House points to foreign travel, foreign lands, and deep intellectual activity.
The fiery element places this rune on the spiritual level
of the microcosm. All of this indicates a soul under
restraint or in servitude seeking escape through physical
travel and intellectual immersion in a specific activity.

The sixth rune is Ansuz (Os), the rune of the wise
and eloquent god Woden himself. It indicates persuasion and wisdom or skill. Mutable Water is the combination of Pisces, the sign of emotionalism, sensitivity,
and an impressionable nature that may express itself in
devotion or self-sacrifice for another person. The
Twelfth House is the house of hidden service and self-
sacrifice, probably in solitude. The watery element
places this rune on the emotional level of the microcosm. This information shows a father figure who is
very eloquent and persuasive, and has stirred a deep
emotional chord in another, awakening a sympathetic
impulse for service and self-sacrifice.

The seventh rune is Laguz (Lagu), which literally
means *water*, but symbolically stands for dreams, the
mysteries of the unconscious mind, and the stirring of
new life. Just as a seed can be awakened by a few drops
of water, so Laguz indicates the awakening of some
hidden impulse or potential. Since this rune stands on
the column of the airy element, this awakening

expresses itself on the intellectual level in the form of communication. Mutable Air is the combination of Gemini, the sign of communication. Gemini often indicates a second marriage. The Third House of Gemini is the house of communications such as telephone conversations, written messages, visiting, and also of mental activities. The interpretation is: the impulse of devotion and self-sacrifice awakened in the previous rune expresses itself on the intellectual level by communication and intellectual activity, but the emotions involved remain superficial.

The eighth rune, Gebo (Gyfu), is the rune of sacrifice or a gift. When a gift is given, it is a gain to the person who receives it but at the same time a loss to the person who gives it away. Also, a gift demands a gift in return to restore the balance of obligations. Mutable Earth is the combination of Virgo, the virgin, the sign of practical and careful service, as well as a coldness in sexual relations. The Sixth House relates to work and service. The earthy element indicates that the gift or sacrifice of Gebo is of a physical or material nature. The interpretation is: a pledge of physical service to another.

The runes of the second cast of the dice relate to the present situation of the woman who is the main subject of the reading. The sense of captivity or servitude (Fehu) in the spirit of the querent's prospective bride is what induced her to sign up for the Mediterranean cruise as a temporary escape. She met the querent, whom she perceived as a father figure (Ansuz). His admiration for her awakened a deep emotional desire in her to dedicate herself in his service (Pisces). However, due to her suppressed emotions, this expressed itself (Laguz) in intellectual playfulness and communications (Gemini) such as e-mail and telephone conversations, rather than any deep feeling of love on her part. It is her intention to devote herself (Virgo) as a gift and sacrifice (Gebo) to the querent. In this role she will be a dutiful but not a sexually passionate partner.

The final cast of the dice reveals the future situation of the querent's relationship with the woman he proposes to wed. In the context of the querent's inquiry, it shows the attitude and condition of the woman during that future time.

The ninth rune is Gebo, sacrifice on the spiritual level in this position, because it stands on the column of elemental Fire. Cardinal Fire is the combination of Aries, the sign of initiative and enterprise. The cross of sacrifice here suggests that the normal energies of Aries will be obstructed, leading to a soul-deadening routine. This will eventually spark some violent reaction. The First House refers specifically to the individual, in this case the person under investigation, the future bride. (Usually the rune in this house refers to the querent.) The sacrifice or gift is spiritual, since it occurs on the fiery column. The interpretation is: spiritual sacrifice through a gift of devotion.

The tenth rune is Isa (Is), literally *ice*. On the symbolic level this rune stands for illusion, seduction, and betrayal. Ice lures the unwary traveler to his doom. Another valid interpretation of this rune is something frozen and unable to change, or be changed. It is the suspension in time of a natural evolution or progression. Cardinal Water is the combination of Cancer, the sign of protectiveness and the maternal instinct. The Fourth House is traditionally the house of the wife and the home. The watery element places this rune on the level of the emotions. The interpretation is: home life results in deception, emotional coldness, and a lack of growth.

The eleventh rune is Eihwaz (Eoh), the yew, a wood associated with toughness, the ability to survive stress and shock, and occult or hidden matters. Since this rune rests on the column of Air, it must be an intellectual toughness. Secrets kept are also indicated. Cardinal Air is the sign Libra, standing for communication between partners or companions, especially between husband and wife. The Seventh House refers particularly to the other person who is the partner in life—in this case, probably the querent, since we are reading the inner nature of his future bride. The interpretation is: words held back, stiffness in the relationship and lack of communication, secrets.

The twelfth and final rune is Nauthiz (Nyd), the necessity to endure hardship. Since it represents the fulfillment of the matter under question, it is a very unfortunate rune in this cast. The marriage, if entered into, will not be happy but will be endured by the woman out of a sense of necessity or duty. Since the rune falls on the column of elemental Earth, physical suffering may be indicated, perhaps even physical abuse. Cardinal Earth is the combination of Capricorn, the sign of the mountain goat. This sign indicates a sense of caution and the perceived need for security, leading to the acceptance of responsibility for practical motives. The Tenth House shows the way the self expresses itself in the outer world. The interpretation is: hardship, suffering, dogged endurance in fulfillment of a perceived duty and also to maintain and protect material security.

If we read up the columns of the elements, we see that on the spiritual level of Fire a father or father figure with very high expectations caused the woman whom the querent wishes to marry to have a low sense of self-worth and to perceive herself as in servitude, which will lead to a sacrifice of the spirit.

On the emotional level of Water, the low self-worth of the woman causes her to experience a deep sense of devotion to the querent when he expresses admiration for her intelligence and abilities. He becomes to her a

substitute for the father she was never able to please.
The result of this misguided devotion of the heart is
deception and emotional frigidity.

On the intellectual level of Air, the woman's penetrating intellect is caught up in a dream of happiness
that has more to do with intellectual compatibility than
true love. The result is the need to conceal her thoughts
and endure the unpleasant shocks of daily life.

On the material level of Earth, the single passion of
the woman's life, her deep love for archaeological investigation and discovery, will be sacrificed due to material
necessities, leading to unhappiness and suffering.

In conclusion, the querent's marriage is likely to
endure, and be a compatible union on an intellectual
level, but it will never result in a truly loving relationship. In the end, it will be maintained merely out of a
sense of obligation, without happiness for either partner. My advice to the querent was that he should seriously consider abandoning his intention to wed this
woman, or at least should put off the marriage for a
year until he knows her better.

# MAGIC AND THE RUNES

## ■——— Ancient Magical Uses

Divination was only one way the runes were used by the shamans of northern Europe. Runes were also extensively employed for practical magic.

One of the powers of the runes mentioned in the Norse *Eddas* and other poems is to speed the process of childbirth. For this purpose runes were cut into the palms of the woman in labor. Her flowing blood nourished them and served as a sacrifice to the rune gods. It was dangerous to use runes in this way, however, because if the wrong runes were cut, they might actually prevent the birth from occurring, and the woman would die in her travail.

The rune master Egil Skalla-Grimsson tells of coming across a rune charm that some well-meaning but ignorant person had placed under the bed of a sick woman. It contained ten runes cut into a piece of whalebone, but what the runes were Egil does not say.

Egil removed the runes, saying that they were prolonging the sickness. He gave this very sensible warning to those who would dabble in rune magic without knowing what they are doing:

> Runes shall a man not score,
> Save he can well to read them.
> That many a man betideth,
> On a mirk stave to stumble.[11]

Runes were called staves, probably because they were originally cut into green saplings, which evolved into the practice of putting the runes on long, slender sticks for magical purposes. Some of these rune wands were elegantly curved and made of yew wood. Bone was also popular for works of magic.

Egil mentions another use for runes. Once while drinking in the mead hall he suspected there might be poison in his drinking horn. He scratched certain unnamed runes into the rim of his horn and stained them with his own blood to empower them. The horn immediately shattered, spilling the wine into the straw on the floor.

The mead hall must have been a dangerous place. In the *Havamal*, Woden describes a charm that protects men from fire. Woden boasts that by the power of this charm, "if the hall blazes around my bench mates,/ though hot the flames,/they feel nought."[12] To understand this reference you must be aware that it was usual for the Norsemen to get so drunk that they could not stand up, let alone flee a burning building. Ancient histories describe instances where groups of men were locked into meeting halls, and the halls set ablaze so that they would all be killed. This was the fabled fate of the followers of Pythagoras, the famed Greek philosopher of the sixth century B.C.

Sailors calmed storms at sea by carving runes into the steering oar of the ship, feathering its edge into shavings with an ax, then setting fire to it. This charm is guaranteed by the author of the *Volsunga Saga* to bring the ship safely back into port no matter how high the waves. This charm is also mentioned by Woden in the *Havamal*, who says: "the wind it calms,/the waves abate,/the sea is put to sleep."[13] For the sea-faring Vikings and Saxons this must have been an important rune charm. The poets do not mention how sailors on the tossing open deck of a dragon ship in the middle of a winter storm in the North Sea could induce a water-soaked oar to burn, but if it was possible, they undoubtedly did it—their incentive was strong.

## Runes and Black Magic

Runes were also employed for overtly occult purposes and to cause misfortune, injury, or death to others. A darker side of the god Woden is hinted at when he tells of a necromantic rune charm he knows that causes the corpse of a hanged criminal to walk and speak. In the *Havamal*, Woden says, "I cut and paint runes,/so the man walks,/and speaks with me."[14] Necromancers consulted corpses because they believed that through the power of magic souls could be induced to temporarily return to their dead and decaying flesh and communicate secrets learned in the land of the dead.

These two stages, cutting the runes and painting the runes, are distinct steps. To cut the runes was to carve or inscribe them into an appropriate surface. To paint the runes was to stain them with fresh blood, which was usually drawn from the magician making the runes. When the runes were cut into the living body of a human being, that person's blood nourished them.

Woden also tells of charms to exorcise and banish troublesome evil spirits or ghosts, and to turn the effects of an evil magic back upon its sender. Rune masters, both male and female, were sometimes sought out to compel the love of individuals against their wills or natural inclinations, or to kill enemies who for various reasons could not be openly attacked.

## Tree-Runes

One technique for working evil by the runes was to carve them into the roots of a living tree below the level of the ground, stain them with blood, then cover them over. Apparently the belief was that as the tree sickened and died, so would the person against whom the magic was directed. The name, and thus the identity, of the victim would have been linked in some manner to the tree by a ritual—by christening the tree in the victim's name, writing the victim's name on the tree with runes, or both. The evil sorcerer may have strengthened this link by burying something from the body of the victim in the earth at the root of the tree, such as hair, nail clippings, excrement, or, if these were not available, a scrap of clothing or a personal possession.

The evil sorcerer probably took measures to ensure that the tree perished, such as cutting its bark in a ring all around its trunk. Very likely the sorcerer made certain the victim learned of the magic, so that he or she would spend the next few weeks watching the tree wither and die. If the bark was cut around the trunk just below the level of the earth, there would be nothing to reveal why the tree was dying. The psychological impact of such a trick would exert a potent effect on the victim's imagination, and would serve to turn the mind of the victim against itself.

Runes were more often employed for constructive purposes, and to heal the sick. The *Volsunga Saga* mentions that bough-runes were used to heal wounds. The runes were cut into the bark and on the buds of trees that faced the east. The thinking behind this practice was that fresh or "green" wounds in the flesh would gradually heal as the runes cut into the fresh, green parts of the tree closed up and healed themselves. In this case, the life force of the tree is used to strengthen a wounded person rather than to weaken a healthy person. The magical principle is the same. It would be necessary to link the tree with the name of the wounded individual, either by naming the tree after the person, or cutting the name of the person into the tree using the runes. Perhaps the link was made stronger by hanging the hair or other intimate products of the person from the boughs of the tree, where they would be warmed by the rising Sun.

## Classes of Rune Magic

There are distinct classifications of rune magic mentioned in the sagas and poems that deal with rune lore. Among these are sea-runes, bough-runes, help-runes, word-runes, thought-runes, book-runes, and taboo-runes. These terms seem to derive from the ways in which the runes were used rather than from any special characteristics of those particular runes or rune charms. Sea-runes were used at sea to calm storms and quiet the waves. Bough-runes were cut into the boughs of trees for healing purposes. Among the help-runes are those already mentioned that were cut on the palms of women in childbirth to speed the delivery of the baby. They are called help-runes because they help.

Word-runes conveyed eloquent speech upon the person who understood how to employ them. These were especially useful in pleading legal disputes. At the *thing*, the tribal council where legal matters were settled, a man was permitted speak in his own defense. (The *thing* was the early beginning of English common law, which still serves as the basic model for much of the modern system of justice used around the world today.)

Thought-runes appear to have granted intellectual power and wisdom to the user. They were employed by priests or magicians who wished to purify their souls or to acquire arcane secrets. Book-runes were likely runes written down as letters to record and convey information. A magician needed the knowledge of book-runes to write down the names of those to whom the power of the runes was directed. Taboo-runes were connected with the word *alu*, which means *taboo*. Alu was employed alone and in combination with runes in numerical sets as a charm to ward off evil, in much the same way that the solitary Algiz rune was used as a charm by common warriors. Taboo-runes would therefore be runes used for an aversive or protective purpose.

## Surviving Scraps of Lore

Usually the runes used in these charms, and the chants that accompanied them, are not known, but occasionally the rune employed is mentioned or implied, or examples of its use have survived. Warriors cut the rune Teiwaz into their own flesh for courage in battle, and carved the rune Algiz into their shields to guard them against the weapons of the enemy. Woden used the "sleep-thorn" to cast the Valkyrie Brynhild into a magical trance. We may conjecture that this was the rune Thurisaz. The legend may have been the origin for the fairy tale of Sleeping Beauty, who fell

unconscious after she pricked her finger on the sharp
spindle of a witch, and who was surrounded by a wall
of deadly and impenetrable thorns while she lay in her
enchanted sleep.

In an Old English poem named the "Nine Herbs
Charm," Woden uses nine "glory-twigs" to kill a serpent:

> For Woden took nine glory-twigs,
> he smote then the adder that it flew apart into nine
> parts.[15]

The adder is probably intended by the anonymous
Christian poet to be the Old Serpent, Satan. A glory-
twig or glory-wand was likely the rune Wunjo carved
into a staff or wand of wood. Nine is a mystical number in Teutonic mythology that is closely associated
with Woden and the runes. On surviving rune relics the
runes sometimes appear in sets of nine. We know that
nine is used in a strictly mystical sense in this poem
because, if a serpent is cut nine times, its body falls into
ten parts, not nine. By repeating the number nine twice
the author stresses its importance in connection with
Wunjo and Woden.

The references above, meager though they are, represent a large portion of what is actually known about
the ancient use of runes for magic. Nowhere in the
sagas or poems or ancient histories is a complete ritual
of rune magic described. Sometimes it is possible to fill
in details of the missing information. For example, in
*Grettis Saga* it is written that to bring disaster on Grettir
a rune witch cuts runes into the scorched side of a drift-
wood tree that still has its roots, then stains them with
her own blood and chants words of doom while walking around the tree widdershins. Grettir's name was
probably written in the runes to link him to the drift-
wood. The uprooted tree, being already dead, served as
a suitable messenger for dealing death.

I mention this scarcity of detailed, factual information on the use of runes for magic so that you will understand how little is actually known about rune magic. After reading some of the books on the magic of the runes that have been written in recent years, you could easily get the impression that we writers know what we are talking about. We do not. We are all guessing. In the best of cases our guesses are based on a careful study of the surviving lore concerning the ancient uses of runes in magic coupled with a broad and practical understanding of magic itself, but they are still guesses.

This is not to imply that modern rune magic is bogus. On the contrary, if correctly constructed it can be incredibly potent. However, it is not identical to the magic used by the Teutonic rune masters, most of which was destroyed and suppressed by the Christian Church, or simply forgotten over time as more and more pagans converted to Christianity and ceased to practice the old ways.

## The Five Stages of Rune Magic

There may be a clue to the ancient system of rune magic preserved in stanza 144 of the poem *Havamal*. In the process of stating what is necessary to know before attempting to use the runes, Woden lists eight magical actions. In my book *Rune Magic* I selected five of these as the essential steps in using the runes for ritual magic, as opposed to using them for divination. These five steps are:

- Cutting
- Staining
- Sending
- Reading
- Evoking

# Cutting

The runes may be cut or inscribed or marked on any surface, even human skin, but there were probably certain rules followed in the process of creating the symbols. They should be cut or marked with firm, confident strokes. Uncertainty in making the runes will greatly weaken their effectiveness, as will untidiness. You should never mark a stroke over and over again. When inscribed in metal with a sharp point or written on paper with a pen, a single line should be used for each stroke. When cut into wood, ideally two passes of the blade of the knife will be enough to remove a thin sliver of material from the groove of the rune.

All of the strokes of the original Germanic futhark were either vertical or diagonal to facilitate their cutting into the green bark of saplings or small tree boughs—there were no curved or horizontal strokes until a later period, when the runes began to be commonly marked on things other than wood. Therefore, use only straight strokes in forming the characters of the futhark, and always mark them in a downward direction. Begin on the left side of the rune and work across to the right side. If the rune has a full-sized vertical stroke that acts as its backbone (such as Teiwaz or Algiz), carve or mark this vertical stroke first, then mark the left side, then the right, working from the top to the bottom. Never cut or inscribe the runes from the bottom of the strokes to the top.

These directions in making the runes are important because occult force flows from heaven to Earth and from left to right, in harmony with the motions of the light from the Sun, which descends from the sky to the ground, and which travels from east to west across the sky (left to right as we face the Sun, for those of us who live in the Northern Hemisphere).

Since the runes were born in the north, it seems appropriate to follow these directions in making them all over the globe. However, those who cut the runes in the Southern Hemisphere would not be wrong in principle if they cut the runes using downward strokes, but worked from the right side of the rune to the left. They would be following the Sun from their reversed perspective. This may seem a trivial matter, but it is a fundamental principle of magic that reflects the basic flow of energy on the planet Earth. Hurricanes rotate counterclockwise in the Northern Hemisphere (as seen from above), but clockwise in the Southern Hemisphere. So do most tornadoes and waterspouts. Similarly, water swirls down a drain counterclockwise in the north, but clockwise in the south. These motions reflect fundamental energy vortices that have their esoteric counterparts.

## Reading

Reading the runes involves a conscious articulation of their names with a complete underlying awareness of their meanings. It is not absolutely necessary to voice the names of the runes aloud to achieve this articulation in the mind, but it is very helpful. After the runes of a work of magic are cut or marked, they should be read in order from left to right, and top to bottom if they occupy more than one row, or clockwise from the top if they are arranged in a circular figure. If the runes are marked irregularly upon a sigil or talisman, read them in their order of meaning so that the reading expresses the collective function of the runes in the ritual.

The purpose of reading the runes is to give them shape on the intellectual level, just as cutting the runes gave them shape on the physical level. Think of cutting the runes as shaping their physical bodies, and reading the runes as naming them, which gives them their

mental bodies. Reading the runes links the physical
and mental bodies of the runes together.

As you name each rune, vibrate the sound of its name inwardly so that to your inner hearing it seems to be voiced in rolling thunder even though the name may be barely a whisper to a person who is next to you. The goal is to have the sound of the names reach the rune gods, who are the potent spiritual forces that animate the runes and give them their power. It is very important that in naming the runes you have a clear understanding of their collective meaning and their magical function.

The most potent way to name the runes is to actually vibrate them on the air. The technique of vibrating names was developed within the Hermetic Order of the Golden Dawn,[16] a magical society that flourished in Victorian England around the end of the nineteenth century. The Golden Dawn is responsible for most of the techniques of practical magic being used in the Western world today.

Put simply, to vibrate a rune you clear your mind of all thoughts and concerns, take a slow deep breath, and visualize the shape of the rune written in brilliant white flames in your own heart center. As you allow the name of the rune to resonate within your chest and throat, imagine your body expanding so that it fills every part of the universe. Imagine that the entire universe is vibrating to the sound of the name, even as your own chest, throat, and nose are vibrating. You must keep your throat open as you articulate the name to allow the column of air within you to resonate freely from your diaphragm to your head.

This takes a little practice, but you will know when you are doing it correctly, because the back of your nose and the bones behind your jaw will vibrate and tickle from the force of the sound. The technique is similar to that used by professional singers and orators to get the maximum clarity and force into their voices.

## Staining

To vitalize the runes and awaken their latent forces the runes must be stained or colored. In ancient times this was done with fresh blood, usually drawn from the body of the shaman for this purpose. The blood acted both as nourishment for the runes and as a sacrifice of something precious from the shaman to the rune gods. Blood was regarded as the seat of vital energy within the body. As God tells Adam:

> *Every moving thing that liveth shall be meat for you; even as the green herb have I given you all things.*
>
> *But flesh with the life thereof, which is the blood thereof, shall ye not eat.*
>
> *And surely your blood of your lives will I require; at the hand of every beast will I require it, and at the hand of every man; at the hand of every man's brother will I require the life of man.*[17]

The meaning of these verses from Genesis is that human beings may eat every kind of flesh, but not drink blood, because the essential life force of a creature resides within its blood. In ancient magic, blood is the life. God jealously reserves the blood for himself. He commands that whenever it is spilled, either by a beast or a human being who kills a beast, or by a human being who kills another human being, it must be spilled as a sacrifice to Him, not consumed by a human being and not sacrificed to any other gods.

Presumably the beasts, who exist in a state of innocence, automatically dedicate the blood of their prey to their Creator, but humankind because of free will is able to keep the blood and use its power for personal purposes. This is the real crime of the mythical being known as the vampire, who drinks blood, and thereby gains immortality, a godlike virtue. In the process the vampire cheats God out of what God regards as His rightful sacrifice.

This prohibition against blood drinking in the Bible shows how common the sacrifice of blood to pagan gods was throughout the ancient world, and why it was performed. The God of the Old Testament is not really saying that it is innately evil to sacrifice blood to other gods, he is saying that he wants all the blood for himself, and if Adam does not give it to him Adam will find himself in serious trouble.

In modern Voudoun it is the practice to feed the drums with the fresh blood of sacrificed beasts. This is done by smearing some of the blood on the drums. The drums are regarded as the vessels of powerful spirits. Unless they are fed with blood, their voices will be weak and lack authority. The impulse that causes Voudoun worshippers to feed their drums with blood is identical to that which caused the Teutonic shamans of northern Europe to feed the runes with blood for acts of magic.

At some early period in the development of runes it probably became common to substitute red earth pigment (red ochre) for fresh blood. In a magical sense red ochre is the blood of the goddess Earth. Runes were often colored red in ancient manuscripts, and in my opinion should never be written for magical purposes in any other color. A scarlet, permanent ink is best when the runes are drawn onto paper or parchment.

Blood-letting is not necessary in modern rune magic, and I strongly discourage its use. The runes should be stained with red ink or paint. Some other fluid of the body, such as saliva, may be used as an alternative. Each bodily secretion has its own occult associations. For example, the occult associations of urine are completely negative. Urine has no place in constructive magic, but was employed extensively in past ages for works of evil. Saliva, on the other hand, is linked with wisdom and cunning speech, and therefore the god Woden.

Two naturally emitted fluids of the body that possess great potency are menstrual blood and semen. Both were used extensively in the magic of the Old World, but because of puritanical censorship the use of menstrual blood and semen in ritual magic is seldom even hinted at, and almost never explicitly described. It is quite likely these fluids were employed by rune masters in ancient times, even though no record of their use has survived.

When the runes are stained, a short prayer should be spoken dedicating the runes, and the ritual in which they are to function, to Woden, the god of the runes. Some small sacrifice should also be made to Woden, either at this time or directly after the ritual. Remember, a gift demands a gift. Use common sense when deciding what you should sacrifice. It could be a donation to charity made in Woden's honor, or an act of self-denial such as giving up a favorite activity for a certain period of time, or breaking some bad habit such as smoking or using profanity. Whatever the form of sacrifice, exercise moderation. What is sacrificed is not nearly so important as the attitude of the person making the sacrifice.

The tendency is to sacrifice something that does not really mean anything, something that you do not truly value. Such attempts to trick the rune gods are unproductive. Anything may be sacrificed, but a sacrifice by its very nature is the giving away of something that you

genuinely value. If you do not value it, then it is not a
sacrifice. Make sure that you actually give the sacrifice
to Woden and the rune gods. This is done by dedicating the sacrifice with a prayer to Woden.

## Evoking

Evoking the runes refers to the rhythmic chants the
shamans recited over them after staining them. These
chants or incantations were extremely important in
ancient rune magic. By their incantations, the rune
masters called forth the rune gods and caused them to
take up residence within the prepared rune symbols.
The chants evoked and awakened the spiritual forces of
the runes. The carving of the runes prepared their physical vessels. The naming of the runes gave them their
individual identities. The staining of the runes provided nourishment for the rune gods. The evocation of
the runes actually places the rune gods within the physical symbols.

Unfortunately, almost all the original rune chants
have been lost. The modern rune magician is forced to
compose original incantations that summon the rune
gods into their symbolic bodies. This is not necessarily
a bad situation. By composing our own calls to the
rune gods, we are certain to completely understand
them and believe in their words. They are less likely to
be recited mechanically, as is often the case when evo-
cations are memorized out of books.

Once these rune forces have been called forth into
our ordinary reality, they can act in the world for magical purposes. They are actualized or manifested by the
chant, which should take the form of a simple rhyming
or alliterative verse that may be spoken over and over,
and resonates in the consciousness and memory like a
verse of poetry, or the verse of a song lyric.

In content, the chant should express the action of the magic the runes are intended to perform. To take a simple example, if you are evoking the rune Algiz (Eolh) to act as the energizing rune on a protective talisman, you might chant the following verse:

> *Eagle's eye and eagle's wing,*
> *Shield me from the serpent's sting,*
> *Hawk's talon and hawk's beak,*
> *Strike the snake and make him meek.*

The shape of the Algiz rune resembles the splayed claw of a bird of prey. The mummified claws of hawks have been discovered in the graves of shamans, indicating that the talons of the hawk were believed to possess magical power, which may have been protective. It is possible that the claw of the hawk or eagle was the original inspiration for the Algiz rune. The serpent is the symbol of the Old Dragon, the Devil, the universal foe of humankind. Birds and serpents are natural enemies.

## Sending

This step in the process of rune magic united the awakened and empowered runes with their target. This might be done by physically placing the rune symbols within the house, upon the land, or even in the pocket of the person they were designed to act upon. If the runes were made for a protective purpose, placing them in the presence of their object would cause them to guard that person from harm. If they were designed to lend some help to the person, their physical union with the person allowed that aid to occur. This is why the runes were actually cut into the palms of a woman in labor, or hidden under the bed of a sick person. On the other hand, if the runes were made to work harm to the person, placing the runes on the person or within the home or place of work of that person caused misfortune to occur.

Sometimes it was impossible to actually put the physical runes into the same physical space as the object or individual they were intended to act on. In this case it was possible to send the runes through the four elements. For example, when the Vikings used runes to calm the winds of a storm at sea, they cut them into the steering oar (symbolizing the sea) and then burned the oar to release the runes into the air (place of the winds). Runes can be sent through Fire by burning them; through Water by casting them into the ocean, a river, a lake, a spring, or a well; through Air by tearing the paper upon which they are written into small pieces and casting it into the wind; or through Earth by burying the runes.

A method of sending the runes should be selected that is symbolically appropriate. For example, Air is the element associated with communication and intellect. Runes intended to influence the thoughts of another person would be sent by the wind, if it was impossible to actually place the runes in the presence of the other individual. (It is always best to physically unite the runes with their object.) Runes intended to attract money would be buried, since money is associated with physical possessions, and Earth is the material element.

One way of sending the runes without actually sending them is to magically identify an object with the subject, thing, place, or person upon which you wish the runes to act. This is a common technique of magic. The best example of its use is the witch doll, or poppet. A doll made in the image of a person, christened in the name of that person, and linked to the person by some intimate physical material such as the person's clothing or hair, serves as a substitute for that individual. If such a doll is made, and the runes are attached to the doll or inserted within the doll, they act just as effectively as they would if physically delivered to the person represented by the doll.

Poppets do not need to represent human beings or be made in a human shape. They can be fashioned to represent a situation, a business, a building, a location, a legal contract, or any other matter. A shape should be chosen that is in harmony with the subject of the magic. For example, if the runes are to be sent to a house that cannot be directly reached in person or through some other agency such as the postal service, the poppet may be made in the shape of a miniature house and the runes placed inside it. This works well, provided the poppet is clearly identified with the thing is represents.

## The Greatest Virtue of the Runes

By using these five simple steps, anyone can work rune magic with little preparation and no special materials. This is one of the greatest virtues of the runes. Because they are symbolic shapes and concepts, not physical objects, they can be carried anywhere in the mind, and made on anything with almost any instrument. No one can take them away from you once you have learned their meanings and the ways of using them. It is not necessary to construct elaborate ritual instruments, collect obscure substances, or buy costly tools when working rune magic. Runes have always been a system of magic for the common people.

# RUNE DICE CHARMS

## ■ ——— Purpose and Function

It is possible to employ the rune dice for magic as well as for divination. In divination, the diviner invites the rune gods to communicate through the runes of the cast, then conveys the revealed information to the querent, who uses it to determine future actions. In rune magic the magician speaks to the rune gods through the dice, using them to direct the rune gods to accomplish specific purposes. In divination we receive, in magic we project. The dice act as a kind of psychic telephone capable of transmitting messages in both directions.

To derive a rune charm from the dice, first it is necessary to know very clearly what purpose you want it to achieve. The charm will be more effective if you create it for a specific function. For example, it is better to make a charm to protect a certain house or a particular person than it is to make a general charm of protection, which unless it is limited in some way will try to protect everything from everything, and so it will accomplish nothing. It is even better to make the charm to protect against a specific type of threat, such as lightning strikes or floods or hurricanes. The more specific the purpose of the charm, the more effectively it will work.

As a rule of thumb, when using the dice for magic, always be very explicit about what you want the rune charm to do, but never try to tell the runes how to do it.

Just the opposite is true concerning the functioning of a rune charm. The more specific and limiting your stipulations about how the charm must accomplish its function, the less potent it will be. For example, if you make a charm to protect a house against a flood, and then stipulate during its making that it must accomplish its purpose by preventing the water from overflowing the banks of the nearby river, the charm is less likely to work because it must overcome the natural forces of the weather for a large area up-river.

Where possible, do not require that a work of magic defy or negate natural processes of nature. These possess a large amount of momentum, in a magical sense, and are difficult to stop or turn aside. When you work magic for a deliberate purpose, and specify nothing concerning how that purpose shall be accomplished, you leave the method of its fulfillment up to the rune gods, who will then choose the easiest way to accomplish their appointed task. For example, if you ask them to protect your house against flood, they may enable you to claim the full amount on your flood insurance so that you can repair the water damage to your house after a flood has taken place, rather than actually stopping the flood itself. Or they may enable you to obtain a powerful pump that will keep the water level in your basement low enough to prevent serious damage.

# You Are an Instrument of the Runes

After you have created the charm, remain open to signs that the charm is working and be prepared to help in the fulfillment of its purpose. Magic always seeks the simplest and easiest method for its fulfillment. Often the easiest way for the rune gods to accomplish a task is to bring about a set of circumstances that enable you to accomplish it yourself. Just because it is magic does not necessarily mean that it is going to be easy for you.

If you want a certain thing to happen, and the runes create a condition wherein you are able to make your wish come true by your own effort, yet you sit back and wait for the runes to do the work for you, the opportunity will pass and you will get nothing. You must understand clearly what you want, work the magic with as much skill and dedication as you possess, then be alert to seize the first opportunity that arises for you to aid in the fulfillment of your purpose.

The runes use everyone and everything as tools to accomplish their works. Since you are the individual who created the charm, you are probably the person most intensely interested in its fulfillment. This makes you a very effective instrument that the rune gods can use to accomplish the task they have been given. If you refuse to allow the runes to use you to achieve your own purpose, you are hindering them in a significant way, perhaps so much so that the charm will become impotent and fail completely.

## Conceiving Your Purpose

The first step in making a rune charm is to think about what you want to accomplish. You may find that your thoughts are confused or contradictory when you actually try to express your wish in words. Try to get to the root of the matter; do not be distracted by superficial circumstances. Isolate in your mind the essential problem or situation that is causing you concern, the one that will make everything else work itself out if only you can solve it.

Once you have conceptualized the purpose of the charm, write it down as concisely as possible. Ideally this statement of purpose should be no more than half a dozen words or so. For example, if you make a charm to protect yourself from getting mugged or attacked, you might state its purpose as "Protect _____ against attacks." (Your own name would appear in the blank.) This would create a general charm of protection, since no specific person has been named from whom you seek protection. If, on the other hand, a woman recently divorced wished protection from her ex-husband who has been following her around and threatening her, she might express her purpose as "Protect _____ against attacks from _____."

## Cutting the Runes

After having written down your purpose as concisely and as explicitly as possible, transcribe it into runes. You can do this by using the equivalents in the Latin alphabet for each rune character. The Fehu rune stands for f, the Uruz rune stands for u, the Raido rune stands for r, and so on. Latin is the alphabet used for writing English, French, and other major European languages. The Latin transliterations for the Germanic runes appear in chapter three. They are not always phonetically accurate, but are very useful in practical magic.

Two runes, Thurisaz (*th*) and Inguz (*ng*), each stand for two Latin letters. Thurisaz should be used to replace *th* and Inguz should replace *ng* or *ing* in the statement of purpose. Each of the other runes replace only a single letter at a time, although several runes stand for more than one individual Latin letter. For example, Wunjo stands for both *v* and *w* individually, and should be used wherever these letters appear in the statement.

Write these runes in a circle on a small piece of paper, starting at the top of the circle and progressing clockwise. Leave the middle of the circle of rune letters empty. Be sure to use bright red ink or paint to mark the runes. After you have written the circle of runes, you can cut it out of the sheet of paper. This paper disk will act as the physical basis for the charm.

If you want to do a more attractive job, the runes may be written within the borders of two concentric circles, the smaller one around an inch less in diameter than the larger circle. These circles can be drawn with a drafting compass in black ink. If you do not own a compass, you can simply use the rims of two glasses of unequal sizes as a guide for your marker. Exactly how big you should make these circles depends on how many runes you intend to write between them. Approximately four inches diameter for the larger circle and three for the smaller is a good workable dimension.

It is not really necessary to be precise in forming the circle of the runes since this charm is not for display. You are probably the only person who will ever see it. However, it is a good policy to treat any matter connected with the runes with respect and care. If you treat the runes with respect, they are more likely to treat you with respect in return. If you treat them carelessly, as though they do not really matter to you, the runes are likely to respond to your requests with equal carelessness and indifference. Always bear this principle in mind when dealing with the runes. It is prudent to make the rune charm as attractive and as close to perfect as your skill allows.

## Casting the Dice

After you have created the framework for your rune charm, you are ready to give it a vital heart. Set the circle of the runes down on a table in front of you, take up the rune dice and hold them pressed between both palms of your hands close to your forehead. Speak a brief prayer to the god Woden asking him to look with favor upon the creation of your rune charm. Be sure to state the purpose of the charm. Then concentrate intensely on the fulfillment of the purpose for which the charm is being made. It is important that you conceive in your mind the fulfillment of the purpose, not the problem that you are trying to overcome. You can do this by using symbolic mental images that represent in your mind the accomplishment of your purpose.

For example, if you are making a charm to protect you from being mugged on the subway, visualize yourself walking unharmed through the subway station at night, a golden glow of health and happiness surrounding your body, and cheerful and friendly smiles on the faces of everyone you pass. Or instead, you might visualize yourself walking through the subway station in the company of a friendly policeman, or riding in a subway car with a savage and loyal guard dog seated beside your feet. If you are making a charm to protect your house from flood, visualize the house sitting on top of a hill on an island in the middle of the ocean. If your charm is intended to protect your house from lightning strikes, you might visualize it covered in a transparent diamond dome.

When you have filled your mind with images that express the fulfillment of your purpose in some symbolic way, take your joined hands away from your forehead, open them at the top like a book by separating your touching thumbs, so that your palms form a dish shape with the dice upon them. Blow across the dice. Close your hands into a cup and shake the dice between them, then part your hands at the bottom where your small fingers touch and allow the dice to fall onto the charm and spread out across the table. Record the four runes of the cast on the disk of the charm in the order of their distance away from you.

The nearest rune should be written with red ink or red paint at the top of the space inside the circle of the runes of the charm. The second rune of the cast is written on the right side of this space, the third rune at the bottom, and the fourth rune at the left side. Make these four runes at least twice as large as the runes of the circle itself. Orient the four larger runes of the cast on the charm so that the may be read from the point of view of the center of the circle. This should also be the orientation of the ring of smaller runes that express the written message of the charm.

## Reading and Staining

After you have marked the four runes of the cast on the charm, concentrate on each rune in order and vibrate its name. Remember to successively visualize the runes blazing in brilliant white fire in your heart center as you vibrate their names in turn. Feel yourself expand to fill the universe as the vibrated sounds pass between your lips.

When you have vibrated all four central runes, they must be stained, and a sacrifice made to Woden and the rest of the rune gods to empower the charm. The staining can be done by smearing a drop of saliva with the tip of your right index finger in a circle clockwise across these four runes, so that the saliva touches all four runes and connects them together. Tears or sweat may also be used, depending on the nature of the charm. Tears are appropriate for charms made to accomplish loving or compassionate ends; sweat is appropriate for charms designed to do physical things that require labor.

As mentioned in chapter sixteen, I strongly discourage the spilling of blood in modern rune magic. Even though they were common in pagan times, blood sacrifices to the runes are not really necessary. Anything that is of personal value to you may be substituted in place of a blood sacrifice at the time of staining. Money, which is valued by most individuals, makes an excellent sacrifice. Burn a single bill of small denomination, crush the ashes to a powder, mingle a few drops of your saliva (or tears, sweat, or other fluid of the body) with the ash, then use this paste to stain the four central runes on the charm. You do not need to apply all the ash to the charm—a small amount is enough.

The response of the runes is in exponential proportion to the sacrifice made to them. This means that the bigger the sacrifice, the bigger the gift from the runes, but the gift from the runes will always be larger in your own estimation than the sacrifice you have made. The sacrifice acts as a kind of catalyst, and causes a disproportionately large reaction. To put it another way, the sacrifice primes the pump—for a little water given, you get a lot more water in return. You always get more from the runes than you give, from a human perspective, but how much more is determined by how much you choose to sacrifice.

There is not really an imbalance between the sacrifice and the gift because what the rune gods give to you is, to them, of relatively small importance, just as what you give to the rune gods is, to you, of less importance than what you receive from the gods. Each side gives something of lesser worth and receives something of greater value. (When you think about it, the same thing happens in any honest business transaction between human beings. In any transaction, each side believes that what has been gained through the transaction is more valuable than what has been lost. If this were not the case, no exchange would occur.)

## Evoking the Runes of the Charm

After the runes have been stained, they must be evoked using a chant or incantation that expresses the fulfillment of their working. Take a knife, hold it by the handle between both your hands with its point down, and move it in a circular clockwise motion in the air over the charm as you recite in a low voice, or under your breath if others are near who might overhear you, the words of the charm that are written in runes around its edge.

It is a good idea to use the specific words that are actually written on the charm as the evocation of the forces of the runes, because this links the physical charm with the ritual actions and the purpose in your mind for which the charm was created. Continue to repeat these words of the charm over and over in an endless circle. As you do so, concentrate all your willpower on the charm. Try to project the achievement of your purpose into the charm.

Remember, it is important to hold in your mind your purpose already achieved, rather than to think of it as something that you want to achieve in the future.

If you conceive the purpose of the charm as already achieved in the present, it will begin functioning immediately.

As you recite the words of the charm, gradually allow the knife between your hands to spiral inward tighter and tighter until, at a climactic moment that feels right to your own intuition, drop the point of the knife directly onto the center of the charm and allow it to rest there for a few moments, supported upright in your hands. Clear your mind completely. Speak a short prayer to Woden giving thanks for the successful fulfillment of your ritual purpose. This must be spoken with confidence. There should be no doubt in your mind that the charm is correctly made and has been successfully empowered.

## Sending the Charm

Take the paper disk of the charm and convey it to the place of its working. If it is a charm of personal protection, it should be carried on the body of the person it is designed to protect. If it is intended to act on a particular place or object, it should be hidden in that place, or concealed within the object where this is possible.

When it is not possible to actually unite the physical rune charm with the object, place or person it is intended to work on, you may have to send it through one of the four elements. To send the charm through Fire, burn it. To send it through Water, cast it into the sea, a river, a lake, or other body of water. To send it through Air, tear it into small pieces and cast it into the wind; alternatively, you may burn it, collect the ashes and reduce them to a powder, then cast it into the wind. To send the charm through elemental Earth, bury it in some symbolically appropriate location.

Use a good quality paper or parchment, and permanent inks or paints, when making rune charms that are not intended to be sent upon one of the elements. This will ensure that they last for as long as they may be needed. Colors made of vegetable dyes fade in strong light. After a few years charms colored with inks containing these dyes will be so pale, it will be almost impossible to read them. Inks that are not labeled permanent blur and run when the paper they are written on gets wet. If you make the mistake of writing your runes in non-permanent ink on a charm that you wear on your body, you will soon discover that the moisture and warmth of your skin has dissolved the runes into blurry, indistinguishable pink blobs. The same common-sense approach to charm making applies in the choice of paper. Cheap paper turns yellow after only a few years and becomes brittle. Eventually it crumbles to dust. A paper of high quality will last for centuries.

A charm intended to be worn on the body should be made of the best materials you can obtain, and enclosed in a moisture-resistant case. A locket makes an ideal container for a rune charm that is to be carried by a woman. A man can sometimes place a charm behind the back of his watch if the charm is small enough and drawn on thin paper. Or the charm can be laminated and carried in the wallet like a credit card. However it is carried, it must be protected from friction and sweat. The best place is over your heart.

## A Sample Charm

Figure 17.1 (following page) shows a rune charm made to protect a car against traffic accidents. The runes

**FIGURE 17.1.** An example of a protective rune dice charm.
This one protects a car against traffic accidents.

around the edge of the circle are a transliteration of the words "Protect this car from accidents." The four runes in the center are those that turned up in the cast while the maker of the charm concentrated on an image of the car driving along a busy highway without a dent or scratch, surrounded by a golden halo.

You should always use the runes that occur in the cast, even if they do not make immediate sense to you when you try to interpret them in connection with the purpose of the charm. Their selection is the magic component to the charm. These four runes act as a key or signature that links the physical charm with the occult forces that will make it effective.

As I mentioned in the chapter on divination by multiple casts, there is a limit of 1,296 possible combinations that can turn up in any single cast of the dice, and these combinations are determined by the underlying structure of the dice themselves. This number of variables is large enough that for any given matter to which the runes may be applied, their action will always be specific and appropriate.

The four cast runes in the example can be interpreted to mean protection and victory (Teiwaz) during personal travel across land (Raido), without transformation or change (Isa), and without danger or hidden pitfalls (Dagaz).

Teiwaz was the rune warriors cut into their own flesh, and into their swords and spears, to ensure courage and victory in a coming battle. In a sense, when we venture onto the highway in our cars we are entering into a dangerous test of courage and skill. If we fail this test our deaths may be the result. Raido literally means riding, or a journey by horse, which in ancient times was the way to travel overland for long distances. The modern equivalent to the horse is the automobile. Isa by one interpretation indicates a lack of change. When we think of our cars, this is exactly what we want—no change in their condition or appearance. We want them to remain just as they were the day we bought them from the car dealer. Dagaz means the light of day, and is a rune of good fortune that banishes fears and dangers.

It is not always possible to interpret the four runes of the cast so meaningfully in the context of the purpose for which the charm is made, but because of the way these runes are evoked during the cast, they will always have significant meaning to the forces of the runes that operate in the functioning of the charm. For this reason you should trust the runes that occur in the cast, even if you do not fully understand them.

# THE RUNE GODS

## ■——The Existence of Rune Gods

Throughout this book you have seen me refer to the rune gods. You will not find mention of these gods in most other books about the runes because their existence is not widely recognized. The majority of academics who study the runes regard them as merely a form of alphabet for writing which may or may not have been used for purposes of magic. Few scholars are willing to admit that magic was the primary function of the runes, and writing was merely a later secondary application.

No one would argue that some of the runes stand for certain gods and spirits. Teiwaz is certainly intended to symbolize the god of oaths and battle, Tyr or Tew. Similarly, Inguz is recognized to stand for the fertility god Ing. Other runes are very suggestive, even though their identification with specific beings is less than certain. Thurisaz is a frost giant or devil, and probably stands for a specific forgotten giant of Teutonic mythology. Ansuz means a god, and is glossed in one place with the name of Woden. Mannaz means more than just man—it stands for humankind as a species, and probably means much the same as Adam, the first man of the Bible.

The remaining runes do not have a clear and definite connection with specific deities. Some stand for trees, some for beasts, some for natural forces, and some for human qualities. The meanings of several runes are ambiguous, which further confuses the whole question.

## All the Runes Are Self-Aware

My contention is that all of the runes were originally understood to embody intelligent and self-aware occult forces that could be manipulated and communicated with by the shamans through the correct use of their runes. In prehistoric times the concept of spirituality was not confined to supernatural entities with the shapes of human beings who live in an otherworldly realm called heaven. This is a later and more civilized view. In the distant past spiritual force and intelligence inhabited everything in the natural world. Trees, springs, rivers, mountains, stones, beasts—all contained gods or spirits of greater or lesser abilities.

It was this perception of the divine in everything that led to the worship of various animal species as the totems of particular clans or tribes. It was also the impulse that caused mountains, springs, lakes, groves of trees, and other natural sites to be worshiped. Originally the beast or place itself was worshiped as a god. In later times it came to be looked upon as the vessel or dwelling place of a spiritual power. Instead of a tree

being a god, a god was thought to live within the tree.
Instead of a mountain being a god, a god was believed
to live on top of the mountain.

In classical times the most important of these
nature gods were abstracted from the elemental forces
that had given them birth, and were cast into the
shapes of human beings. They were regarded as larger
than ordinary mortals, longer of life or deathless, more
beautiful, more powerful, and wiser, but they were still
human in shape and motivation. They wanted what
human beings want, felt what humans feel, loathed
what humans loath, and committed the same errors
that humans commit in their frailty.

It is useful for a people to make its gods human.
When a god exists in the shape of a human being, and
is subject in some limited degree to human needs and
human weaknesses, he or she is more apt to listen with
sympathy to the prayers and appeals of worshipers.
The gods and goddesses of ancient Greece and Rome
were very easy to understand and communicate with.
They may have lived on top of Olympus, but they had
the same drives and desires that tormented their mortal subjects.

However, in making a god human a large portion of
its original elemental wildness and natural potency is
sacrificed. Woden started out as a storm god. He was
the howling wind that tore the clouds across the dark
vault of heaven, and the flashing lightning and rolling
thunder. In this role he brought death and destruction,
and was more to be feared than revered. When he was
cast into the shape of an old man with one eye, he lost
some of this elemental fury. It still remains buried deep
within his essential identity, but it can only be called
upon by those who truly know him.

# Untamed Gods of the Northern Shamans

I believe that in their earliest beginnings all of the runes were gods or goddesses. Some were the spirits of trees, some of the forces of nature, some of totemic beasts, and some of the forces that work within the nature of human beings. When the runes are recognized as living gods, as the ancient shamans knew them to be, they are more potent agents in works of divination and magic. We who use the runes for these purposes have good reason to restore their original identities. The greater the inherent power of the runes, the greater their usefulness.

It is impossible to know exactly which gods or spirits the runes originally represented, but by analyzing their meanings it is possible to arrive at a general concept of the natures and purposes of these shamanic deities. The following descriptions of the rune gods should give you a more complete concept of the runes. They will also help you to interpret them in your divinations and use them more effectively in your rune charms.

## Fehu

The goddess Fehu was probably a cattle deity. Cow goddesses are common in many ancient cultures. The Egyptians worshiped the cow in the form of the goddess Hathor. Primitive life in Europe revolved around the management of cattle. They were considered more precious possessions than human slaves. Since cows provide milk that is drunk or made into cheese, meat for the table, hide that is made into leather, manure for the fertility of the crops in the fields, and bone that has numerous practical functions, cow goddesses are deities of nurture and benevolence. Fehu was probably called upon by those who sought to increase the size of their cattle herds, the measure of wealth in pagan times. It may well have been a rune of good fortune.

## Uruz

This masculine god was the collective totemic spirit of the aurochs. It probably served some of the functions of the bull gods of Egypt, which symbolized strength, fierceness, and virility. Even though the cow and the bull are opposite sexes of the same species, they have very different identities in magic, and were represented by different gods in Egyptian mythology. Cow gods are benevolent, gentle, and nurturing; bull gods are fierce, violent, and dangerous.

The aurochs was a large beast with black shaggy hair and curling horns that resembled a large ox. In his *Gallic Wars* Julius Caesar describes it as somewhat smaller than an elephant with an appearance similar to a bull. He says that the aurochs attacks any man or beast it sees, and that it is impossible to tame even if caught at a young age. Young German men tested their manhood by hunting it with spears and dogs, and driving it into pits to kill. The horns were rimmed with silver and used as drinking cups at banquets in the mead hall of the chief. They were exhibited with great pride as trophies that proved the skill and courage of the hunter.

In earliest times hunting the aurochs probably represented some formal or semi-formal trial of manhood. In later centuries this degenerated into mere sport. The last remaining aurochs were hunted to extinction during the seventeenth century. For the pagan Germans the aurochs must have been the most potent and important of all totemic beasts, equivalent to the bison for the American Plains Indians. It represented the essence of courage and freedom, and thus manhood. When a boy became a man, he ceased being subservient to the will of another and began to rule his own destiny.

It is likely that the god of the aurochs was larger than the normal beast in stature, and pure white in color. Albino mutations occur in most animal species—there are white buffalo, white tigers, white bears, white apes, and so on. These white beasts were usually regarded as divine by the human population who lived in close contact with the species to which they belonged.

## Thurisaz

The god of this rune probably arose from a baleful aspect of nature that through fear and awe became personified in the form of a giant. Since there is some slight evidence that this rune is connected with sleep, it is possible that Thurisaz is the giant or demon of darkness. Darkness is symbolically associated with evil, just as light is associated with good.

Thurisaz is a male giant who brings pain, suffering, and sickness to women. The two physical phenomena uniquely associated with women are childbirth and menstruation. The god of this rune probably has power over both functions. Until very recent times in Western culture menstruation was looked upon as a sickness or curse rather than as a natural process of the body. Excessive or painful monthly bleeding in women would have been blamed on Thurisaz. This god would also be blamed for painful and prolonged travails, stillbirths, or the death of women during childbirth.

The association of this rune with the common thorn bush in the *Old English Rune Poem* may simply result from the fact that, when touched, thorns cause pain and bleeding—the same conditions that occur to women during menstruation and childbirth. This may well have been the rune cut into the palms of pregnant women to hasten the birth of their babies. By sacrificing their life blood to the demon or giant Thurisaz, the women appease the demon and obtain a mitigation of the torment he enjoys causing.

From the *Icelandic Rune Poem* we learn that Thurisaz is a cliff-dweller, and the husband of Varthrun (Vardhrúnar), presumably a giantess. Varthrun may be an alternative name for one of the other runes, but if so it has not been identified. The third rune of the second aett is Isa, which falls directly below Thurisaz when the aettir are written out in three lines from left to right. Isa would be an appropriate mate for Thurisaz. Another possibility is Perth, which falls directly below Thurisaz when the futhark is written in three lines *boustrophedon*, that is, back and forth the way a farmer ploughs a field. This rune would make an interesting contrast as the wife of Thurisaz.

The rune god Thurisaz should be conceived as a giant, shadowy creature of darkness who conceals himself during the day in a deep cave on the side of a cliff, but ventures out at night to cause pain and excessive bleeding in menstruating women, and to hinder the travail of pregnant women whose labor pains extend into the hours of darkness, which is more often the case than not in pregnancies. The god takes delight in causing this suffering. For these reasons the Thurisaz rune was a symbol of bad luck when it occurred in a divination. *The Norwegian Rune Poem* reads: "Thurs causes illness in women;/few rejoice at bad luck."

## Ansuz

This is one of the few runes that is explicitly a god. The *Icelandic Rune Poem* calls Ansuz an ancient creator, the King of Asgard and Lord of Valhalla. *Ancient* probably means original or first in this context—Woden, the creator of gods and men. We can gain an understanding of the essential characteristics of this rune god from the *Norwegian Rune Poem*, where Ansuz appears defined as the mouth of a river. This is said to be "the way of most journeys" but "a scabbard" of "swords."

The meaning of the riddle is that the wisdom of Woden flows in an unending stream of eloquent words from his mouth, like the mighty and uninterrupted flow of waters from the mouth of a river. It is the way of most journeys, because in ancient times most journeys were by river or ocean voyages. There were no roads, so the only other recourse was through forests on horseback, a slow and difficult method of travel. It is a scabbard of swords because eloquent arguments at the *thing* forestalled battles.

Woden has so many forms and attributes that it is difficult to count them all, but the form of the rune god of Ansuz is Woden in his role of father of the gods and men, peace-maker, wise judge, and eloquent counselor. This is a very favorable rune, and was probably viewed as a sign of good fortune when it appeared in a cast.

## Raido

The rune god of Raido is a god of authority and command who rules over the lower aspects of the self, such as the physical needs and emotions, with higher aspects of the seof, such as reason, skill, and self-control. The essential meaning of this rune is riding, or a journey by horse. However, the rune poems emphasize the relationship that exists between the horse and the rider. It is that of a servant and its master. The *Norwegian Rune Poem* comments "riding is said to be worst for horses," meaning worse for the horse than for the man it carries on its back. The *Icelandic Rune Poem* reinforces this concept, saying that riding is a "joy of the rider" but at the same time "laboring of the horse."

The essential notion of this rune is command of the physical weaknesses for the purpose of progress on the road of life. In the *Norwegian Rune Poem* the enigmatic line is added "Regin forged the best sword," which seems to make no sense until we consider that the discipline of the rider (mind) over the horse (body) is a kind of spiritual tempering of the soul. By making our lower passions the horse of our spirit, we progress swiftly to our destination. The rune god of Raido is a god of discipline who is probably associated with some lost quest myth, similar in underlying meaning to the quest for the Holy Grail of the Arthurian legends. This god may be conceived as a mounted knight or spiritual warrior who has a noble and far-seeing nature.

## Kano

The essential meaning of Kano is that of the torch, a source of light. It may be distinguished from the light of the day (Dagaz), which is from the Sun and cannot be controlled or regulated by human beings. Kano is the light of fire, and fire is under the command of humanity. Indeed, in Greek myth and in the myths of other cultures it is the gift of the gods to humankind.

Kano is both the guiding light that directs the quest of Raido, and the prize for successfully completing the quest. In the *Old English Rune Poem* the torch is said to be "known to all the living," that is to say, the spiritually awakened who will ascend into the mead hall of Woden in Valhalla, here contrasted with the spiritually dead, whose souls are dark, and who will be denied entrance to the hall. The poem goes on to say that the torch most often burns inside the hall "where princes sit at ease." This may be interpreted literally, as torches were most often used for light indoors, but it also has a symbolic meaning. The hall is the hall of Woden. The princes are the honored dead, who have fulfilled the quests of their life journeys.

The god of this rune would be someone similar to Baldr (also spelled Balder), the Teutonic god of light who has been compared with Jesus Christ. Baldr is a god of death and resurrection, as is Christ. He is the good ruler who causes harmony and prosperity in the land he rules. His name has been associated by some authorities with bál, which means "shining" or "white," and appears in the word *balefire*, which was both a beacon fire lit atop a high place, and also a funeral fire for consuming corpses.

The rune god of Kano is a shining god of every human being's life journey, spiritual quest, honored death, and blessed resurrection. Baldr is the light of Valhalla. In my opinion the god of this rune may be conceived in the form of Baldr.

## Gebo

The rune god of Gebo is almost certainly connected with the myth of Woden's self-sacrifice on the world tree Yggdrasill. It may be significant that this rune takes the form of a cross. When the human body is held down or bound up for sacrifice with arms and legs extended, it assumes a form similar to Gebo. (However, it is always dangerous to read too much meaning into the shapes of the runes.)

In the *Old English Rune Poem*, this rune is given the purely materialistic interpretation of the generosity of a chief in giving food and other gifts to his landless vassals. However, it is also described as a "means of survival" to the "dispossessed" who have no other way to meet their physical necessities. If the chief is considered to be a god, and the gifts are spiritual gifts necessary to the survival of the soul, then the rune stands for the generosity of the god in providing spiritual nourishment in times when the soul is starved for wisdom and guidance.

The shaman in undergoing the trial of Woden on Yggdrasill deliberately created such a condition of spiritual famine through his extreme physical dedication and suffering. The gift the god Woden gives to the shaman who invokes his aid while suspended from the tree is the wisdom of the runes. Since this gift is given by the Father of humanity to his children, the god of Gebo may take the form of Woden in his role of master of the runes and teacher of a higher wisdom.

## Wunjo

The god of Wunjo is connected with glory or joy, specifically the ecstatic state that follows the rigorous rite of initiation into a wisdom cult or hierarchy. This is the brilliant revelation of some mystical truth that profoundly and permanently alters the awareness of the initiate. Often this transformation is symbolized by the enactment of a drama of death and rebirth. The trial of Woden on the tree Yggdrasill is an example of such a drama. Woden dies on the tree in his old self and is reborn with the power and wisdom of the runes. The mythic death and rebirth of Jesus on the cross fulfills the same function.

In addition to mystical wisdom, Wunjo seems to have signified magical potency. Woden used "glory twigs" to slay the serpent in the Anglo-Saxon "Nine Herbs Charm." Therefore Wunjo is the magical power to subdue and destroy the dragon of darkness. It is interesting that in the "Nine Herbs Charm" the serpent is cut by nine glory wands into nine parts. In a sense, the serpent becomes the wands, or the wands become the serpent. Throughout the ancient world serpents, and their mythical counterparts, the dragons, are associated with higher wisdom, particularly the wisdom of initiation and secret occult societies.

The god of Wunjo may be conceived as a god of wisdom and magical power, similar in function to the gods Thoth of Egypt and Hermes of Greece. Thoth is the sacred scribe who records the judgments of Osiris, the lord of the dead. Hermes is the psychopomp (soul-guide) who escorts the souls of the dead to the underworld. This role was played in Egyptian mythology by Anubis, the jackal god, who was closely linked with Thoth. Both functions are subsumed under the form of the god Hermes Trismegistus, a merging of Hermes with Thoth that took place during the Greek military occupation of Egypt, and endured throughout the subsequent Roman occupation of Egypt.

The symbol of Hermes is the serpent staff, or caduceus, which is still used today as an emblem of the medical profession. The serpents on the staff portray in a single image the meaning in the verse of the "Nine Herbs Charm." The rune wand of Wunjo (the staff) divides the dragon of darkness or chaos (on the caduceus the division is into two, male and female, the powers of creation) and thereby takes on the wisdom and magical power of the dragon (symoblized by the wings on top of the staff). The wand rules the serpents, and by assuming their magic, it becomes the serpents (see Exodus 7:10–12).

## Hagalaz

There is a fairly clear mythological creature that serves to embody the rune god of Hagalaz—the frost giant. In Teutonic mythology, giants were associated with weather phenomena, mountains, the sea, and other expressions of the powers of the natural world. The

frost giants were spirits of the winter storms. Hagalaz
literally means *hail*. This was an evil rune because no
good came from hail. It could destroy an entire crop in
the field just before the day of its harvest, and in
ancient times the loss of a year's crops often meant starvation for the community, or, at the very least, consid-
erable hardship.

In the *Old English Rune Poem* hail is called "the
whitest of grains," a metaphor intended to link it in the
mind of the reader with the destruction of crops. It is
very interesting that the *Icelandic Rune Poem* describes
hail as the "sickness of serpents." This points to a link
between this rune and the serpent, with its numerous
symbolic associations, but does not reveal the nature of
the link. Perhaps hail was considered to be the frozen
vomit of serpents or dragons, which was cast down
upon the Earth to blight it.

The rune god of Hagalaz may be conceptualized as a
fierce giant whose hair, beard, and eyebrows are covered
in white frost, and who scatters hailstones from his fin-
gertips. His voice is the roaring wind of a winter storm.
A bone-chilling cold emanates from his body and
freezes everything around him. His nature is violent and
destructive. It is impossible to reason with this god.

## Nauthiz

In its most mundane sense, this rune signified the service that must be paid by a vassal or serf to his chief or
lord. It is translated as the necessity to endure. The
more general meaning is of need or want. The *Norwegian Rune Poem* states "need leaves little choice;/the
naked man is chilled by the frost." By this image Nauthiz is connected with the preceding rune Hagalaz. The
*Icelandic Rune Poem* calls need the "distress of bondwomen" and a "state of oppression and hard labor."

Why specifically a distress to bondwomen rather than bondmen? Perhaps the need to endure unwanted sexual relations or unwanted pregnancy is intended.

By linking need to nakedness, the poet of the *Norwegian Rune Poem* shows that the suffering of Nauthiz was connected in ancient times with the loss of property. A man or woman without wealth or possessions suffered need. An essential interpretation of this rune in a cast would be the suffering that results from the loss of something important.

The *Old English Rune Poem* gives a much more complex interpretation to this rune, which may have been influenced by Christianity. Although it calls need or hardship an "oppression of the heart," nonetheless it introduces a note of hope, saying "often it is transformed for the sons of men/to a source of help and salvation, if only they heed it in time." Suffering becomes a divine instrument for teaching spiritual wisdom.

A useful way to perceive the rune god Nauthiz is as a spirit of famine, who has ragged clothing or is completely naked, and whose body is gaunt and thin, with the bones close beneath the stretched skin. Anyone who has seen the remarkable statue of the Buddha as a starved, ascetic monk, the artist Grünewald's painting of Christ taken down from the cross, or the photographs of the survivors of the Nazi death camps, will understand how an image of extreme human suffering can sometimes also be an image of spiritual endurance and strength. Nauthiz is both the need to endure and the will to endure.

## Isa

This rune literally means ice, and its deity is best perceived as a beautiful but evil goddess who seduces travelers to their doom by luring them out on the ice of rivers, lakes, or the sea. In the *Old English Rune Poem* ice is described as extremely cold and slippery, but is also said to be "like jewels" and "fair to behold." The *Norwegian Rune Poem* refers to ice as "the broad bridge" and adds the enigmatic line "the blind man must be led." The *Icelandic Rune Poem* conveys much the same information, calling ice the bark of rivers and the roof of the wave, indicating that river-ice and sea-ice are both intended, then adds that it is "destruction for doomed men."

From these poetic hints we may gather that the goddess Isa is an alluring seductress who tempts travelers to take the easy way across the smooth, open expanse of rivers, lakes, or sea inlets rather than the more difficult irregular journey over frozen, snow-covered ground. She leads men blinded by the prospect of swift travel to their doom.

In ancient times, the temptation to travel across the surface of rivers and lakes during winter months when the water was locked under ice must have been great, particularly since these bodies of water were the normal highways when not frozen. Anyone who tested their luck too far by continuing to use frozen rivers or sea inlets in the spring risked being caught out on a stretch of rotten ice and falling through. This still occurs today, but must have been even more common in the past when there was no other convenient method of travel except across the ice.

Because water has always been associated in mythology with Undines, spirits who are usually depicted as beautiful women who tempted men to their doom beneath the surface, it is natural to imagine the goddess Isa as a beautiful Undine of the winter who ensnares travelers by luring them out on the ice, then trapping them beneath its surface in her chill embrace. In some ways she is similar to the goddess of the underworld,

Hel or Hela, who is also a fatal beauty. For the ancient Teutons the land of Hel was dark and cold, a contrast to the torch-lit warmth of Valhalla, Woden's hall of heroes.

## Jera

This rune refers in its narrow sense to the time of harvest, which was understood to be the year's end. In a broader sense it means the year. The god Jera would be some form of harvest deity, and would have the familiar qualities of joviality, generosity, drunkenness, and excess that we associate with other harvest gods such as Bacchus. In the *Old English Rune Poem* Jera is called a "joy to men." The *Norwegian Rune Poem* echoes this sentiment, calling Jera a "boon to men," while the *Icelandic Rune Poem* says it is a "blessing to men," and also says that it signifies "a good summer/and fully ripe crops." This is probably the basic interpretation of this rune when it occurs in a cast.

A useful concept for this rune god is that of a fat, jovial, somewhat drunken spirit. The early forms of Father Christmas or Santa Claus serve as good models for the god of Jera. The Greek Dionysus or Roman Bacchus also make useful models. For the ancient Teutons, beer was the important alcoholic drink rather than wine, so the god of Jera would be a beer god rather than a wine god. If this rune god is imagined in female form, a cheerful form of the Roman goddess Ceres would be most appropriate.

The capricious, occasionally dangerous aspect of Santa Claus is applicable here, because the harvest is not always a happy season. Before Santa Claus became a brain-dead fat man, he was an expression of Loki, the trickster, and could be capricious or even malicious when the mood struck him. If the frost or hail comes before the crops can be taken in from the fields, harvest season is a time of woe and loss. This is why Jera may

be associated with change, inversion, or fate. The year is
a wheel of fortune—sometimes when it spins it gives a
plentiful bounty from the earth; at other times its harvest is bitter and cold. This hard edge in the character
of the rune god of Jera should always be retained.

## Eihwaz

It would be difficult to state with certainty why the yew
tree is associated with the dead. Yews are very long of
life. Probably graveyards became associated with yews
when Christian churches were erected on the sites of
ancient pagan temples, many of which were surrounded by groves of yews. The yew is an evergreen. Its
continuing greenness in the midst of the snows of winter may have suggested to the pagans that it was
endowed with a greater than usual amount of life force.

The roots of the yew were fabled to reach down into
the land of the dead. In fact, they did extend into the
rotting coffins of buried corpses. The fertilizer for
churchyard yews was strange indeed! This unsettling
notion of yews feeding on the bodies of the dead probably contributed to their association with ghosts and
other restless spirits. In pagan times, trees were
regarded as the residences of spiritual beings. It would
be natural to look upon the yews in churchyards as
receptacles for the spirits of the dead.

The most important use for the yew was to make
bows, particularly the famous English longbow. Like the
ash, which was used for the shafts of spears, the yew was
a wood associated with warfare. The *Icelandic Rune Poem*
makes specific reference to this use when it calls the yew
"bent bow/and brittle iron/ and giant of the arrow." The
reference to iron may be to the arrow points.

Another more curious association that occurs in the
rune poems is the link between the yew and fire. The
references suggest that the burning of yew wood may

have had some ritual function. In the *Old English Rune Poem* yew is described as a "keeper of flame." The *Norwegian Rune Poem* adds the comment "when it burns, it sputters." Because we know it was the custom of rune magicians to make rune charms out of short yew wands, it is possible that these charms were activated by ritually burning them. It also may be that the ritual burning of yew, spurred by the fact that yew remains green all winter, had some unknown cult purpose, and by association all yew wood was linked with fire and its vital energies. This would have made it a potent material upon which to cut runes.

Eihwaz was probably looked upon as a generally favorable rune when it turned up during divination, since the *Old English Rune Poem* calls yew "a keeper of flame" and "a pleasure to have on one's land." On the basis of these and other hints, I have associated Eihwaz with dependable strength and vitality, in addition to linking this rune to the spirits of the dead (because yews grow in graveyards) and to warfare (because yew wood was made into war bows).

How the god of this rune is conceived depends on which of these three meanings is considered to be most prominent. Underlying all the associations of the yew is its inner vitality, which was thought to make the tree long of life and green in the winter, to give it strength and flexibility for bows, and to cause it to sustain a fire for a longer than usual span of time. The god of Eihwaz would be a spirit of the secret or hidden life force. One possible form such a deity might assume is a ball of crackling fire, similar to the Will O' the Wisp that is associated in folklore with ghosts and spirits. Other natural phenomena with the same associations are St. Elmo's Fire and ball lightning. There is a folk superstition that the appearance of ball lightning foreshadows a death.

The god Loki was originally a fire spirit. In Scandinavia when a fire crackles they say that Loki is beating
his children. This may be a very distant echo of the ritual practice of burning yew. It is possible that yew is
connected with Loki. You may wish to conceive the
rune god of Eihwaz as a fiery form of Loki.

## Perth

Any speculation about the nature of the god of this rune
is limited by the complete lack of solid information
concerning its meaning. I have conjectured that Perth
means the apple tree, with the accompanying symbolic
associations of its wood and fruit. Apple wood was
probably used from earliest times to cut runes upon for
divinations. At a later, more decadent period of rune
magic, apple wood probably formed the basis for rune
lots that were used for gambling in the mead halls. It is
even possible that these gambling lots were dice.

Perth has the associations of luxury and sin (from
the fruit of the apple), prescience and fate (from the
use of apple wood in divination), and chance and luck
(from the use of apple wood for gambling lots). I tend
to emphasize the first of these meanings in my own
interpretations of this rune. The connection between
these three very different meanings is the ancient use
of apple wood as the basis for rune staves. This use is
conjectured but not proven. Of all the runes of the
futhark, Perth is the most mysterious. Everything said
about this rune is guesswork. This applies to what I
have said about it, and to what every other writer on
the runes says about it.

I prefer to conceive the deity of Perth as a beautiful
goddess who is sensual and pleasure-loving—in Norse
mythology the goddess Freyja. This goddess is a member of the race of gods called the Vanir, not the Aesir to
which Woden and the other more familiar gods of the

North belong. It is said that she taught witchcraft (*sei-dhr*), was by nature greedy and lascivious, and should be invoked in matters of love. She also delighted in pornographic love poetry. She is similar to the Roman goddess Venus.

## Algiz

This rune has the shape of a hawk's foot. We know this shape has some meaning because in connection with this rune in the *Norwegian Rune Poem* appears the enigmatic line "great is the claw of the hawk." Among the Norse runes this rune has been given the name and meaning of man, while the original Germanic rune for man has disappeared. However the reference to the claw of a hawk clearly refers to the shape of the rune.

In the *Old English Rune Poem*, the meaning of this rune is elk-sedge, a tough, fibrous grass that grows in marshes. The symbolic meaning of defense or taboo has persisted. The poet says about elk-sedge that it "gives grievous wounds,/Staining with blood every man/who lays a hand on it." This seems a rather extreme thing to write about a kind of grass. It would be more appropriate to the claw of a hawk, and in my opinion the hawk's claw is the original literal meaning of this rune.

It was possible to transfer the meaning to elk-sedge because, when an attempt is made to pull up a bunch of shoots of this tough plant, its stalks part into networks of tough, sharp fibers that can cut into the skin. I have had this experience myself as a boy when trying to uproot fistfuls of marsh weeds. The cuts are very painful.

The hawk must have been an extremely powerful totem for the shamans of the Old World, just as it was for the shamans of the New World. Mummified claws of hawks have been found in graves that are likely the graves of shamans. These claws were probably used ritually as power objects, perhaps for warding off or banishing evil or dangerous spirits, or for driving out the spirits of disease. We will never know their exact use, since this information has been lost over time.

The rune god of Algiz should be conceived as the spirit of the hawk. An appropriate form is that of a larger than normal hawk with white feathers that is capable of human speech. This type of talking animal totem is known to Teutonic mythology. Woden had two ravens, named Huginn and Muninn, that followed him everywhere and told him secrets of distant places. Woden was also believed able to transform himself into the form of a raven, along with other animals. The feathers of the hawk or eagle symbolized spirit flight for shamans.

## Sowelu

This rune formed the basis for the infamous double lightning bolt insignia of the Nazi SS. It may originally have signified the flaming streak of a meteor across the heavens. In the rune poems it has come to mean the solar ray, which is associated in the *Norwegian Rune Poem* with divine judgment. In the *Icelandic Rune Poem* the shining ray from the Sun is said to be the "destroyer of ice," which is interesting when we consider the symbolic meanings for Isa, among them treachery, deceit, illusion, entrapment, and doom. Ice also suspends the natural processes of life. These are restored by the ray of Sowelu.

The Tarot trump called the Blasted Tower accurately expresses the essential meaning of Sowelu. This card illustrates a bolt of lightning streaking down from the orb of the Sun to strike and destroy a tall tower, which is probably intended to represent the Tower of Babel.

The tower is humankind's corruption, disobedience, and self-delusion. The lightning bolt is the judgment of God.

The rune god of Sowelu is a wielder of the thunderbolt. In Norse mythology, Thor is the god of lightning, symbolized by his hammer. His hammer is represented by the ancient symbol the swastika—two Sowelu runes crossed over each other. The swastika is essentially a solar symbol. Thor is the defender of order against chaos. He battles the Midgard worm or dragon (Mithgardhsorm), symbol of chaos. The Romans identified Thor with their own thunder god, Jupiter. Thor in his role of wise and just defender of the world against chaos is a useful form of the god of Sowelu.

## Teiwaz

This is one of the few runes that is explicitly named after a well-known Teutonic god. Tew (also spelled Tiw) or Tyr (Also spelled Tir) was the god of oaths and legal contracts. His nature is best expressed in the story of the wolf Fenrir. The wolf was raised from a cub by the Aesir, but only Tyr was brave enough to feed him. Having foreknowledge of the future harm Fenrir would inflict upon the gods, Tyr decided to chain the wolf, but Fenrir was so powerful he broke the first two chains that were put on him. The third chain was dwarf-forged and impossible to break. By this time Fenrir had grown wary of the gods. He agreed to allow himself to be chained, supposedly as a test of his strength, only if one of the gods would place his hand in the wolf's mouth as a pledge. No god but Tyr had the courage to fulfill this demand. When Fenrir realized that he had been tricked, he bit off Tyr's hand and ate it. Thenceforth Tyr was known as the One-handed, just as Woden was called the One-eyed.

This story illustrates the great courage of Tyr, which was his most admired quality by the warriors of the North. Originally he was an honored and powerful god of the *thing*, the tribal assembly at which disputes were settled and judgments delivered. He was before all else the god of honor and truth. In later centuries, Tyr became overshadowed by the cults of Woden and Thor. He was remembered only as a great warrior, and his rune was used as a talisman by men about to go into battle to provide strength and courage. The Romans identified Tyr with their own war god, Mars.

In the *Old English Rune Poem*, Tyr seems to be equated with the North Star. He is called one of the "guiding signs" that "keeps faith with princes" and always "holds its course above the night clouds." To emphasize the point the poet adds the words "it never fails." The references in the other rune poems are more enigmatic. In connection with this rune the poet of the *Norwegian Rune Poem* adds the riddle "often has the smith to blow." In order to keep a fire hot enough to soften iron, blacksmiths had to regularly force fresh air over the glowing embers with a bellows. Perhaps the virtues of Tyr, courage and honor, are being equated with the fire of the furnace. In the *Icelandic Rune Poem* Tyr is described as the "leavings of the wolf/and king of temples." The first reference is clear enough, but the second is obscure. It may be that Tyr fulfilled some sort of function as the guardian spirit of holy places.

The wolf was probably the totemic beast of Tyr. The story of his voluntary sacrifice of his hand was a way of indicating Tyr's connection with the wolf, who would be expected to watch over and protect Tyr's worshippers. The chaining of the wolf also shows that this god expresses the power of law and order over chaos. His role is similar to Thor's in this matter. Both Fenrir the wolf and the Midgard serpent are agents of chaos who make war against the gods, the agents of order.

## Berkana

The birch tree is the literal meaning of this rune. The birch is associated with the rites of spring because it was the first tree in the northern forests to turn green after the long winter. There are numerous pagan uses of birth twigs to promote fertility both in animals and in human beings. The Scandinavian practice of lashing the body with birch wands while taking a sauna probably goes back to some forgotten fertility rite.

The *Icelandic Rune Poem* calls the birch a "little tree/and youthful shrub" to emphasize its connection with the newly awakened life of springtime. The tree itself is represented as newly born. In the *Norwegian Rune Poem* appears the riddle "Loki was lucky in his deception." This probably refers to a story that Loki changed himself into a flea and bit the sleeping goddess Freyja on the cheek, causing her to roll over, so that he could steal her precious dwarf-forged necklace for Woden, who was outraged at the way Freyja had obtained the jewelry. In order to induce the four dwarves who made the necklace to part with it, Freyja had gone to bed with each of them in turn.

Freyja, the sister of the fertility god Freyr and a member of the Vanir, was said to be Woden's mistress or his wife. She is frequently confused with the more chaste mother goddess, Frija or Frigg, a member of the Aesir who is also supposed to be Woden's wife. Frigg was occasionally unfaithful to Woden, when it suited her purposes, but never as promiscuous as Freyja. Because the rune Berkana is mainly concerned with sexuality as a source of fertility and new life, as opposed to sexuality as a source of sensual pleasure, it would be appropriate to make Frigg or Frija, the lawful wife of Woden, the goddess of this rune, just as the Vanir goddess Freyja, who is always seeking to satisfy her own desires, is the deity of the rune Perth.

## Ehwaz

This rune literally means a horse. The god Ehwaz would be another totemic deity, a white horse of unearthly intelligence, grace, endurance, and speed that possesses the gift of speech. An ideal candidate for this role would be Woden's horse, Sleipnir, except for his color. He was a gray stallion with eight legs, the finest of all horses. Runes were carved upon his teeth. He possessed the ability to gallop over the waves of the sea or across the clouds.

Gray is the color of death. The horse had a close association with death in Teutonic mythology. The tree from which Woden hung suspended in his quest for the runes is sometimes called Sleipnir ("Woden's Horse"), and the gallows was kenned "the high-chested rope-Sleipnir." The Death Goddess was referred to as the "Valkyrie of the horse." Hundreds of horse graves have been unearthed throughout Scandinavia. However, death is not a major factor in the rune Ehwaz, so the god of this rune should be conceived as a snowy white stallion.

In the *Old English Rune Poem* the horse is simply described as the "joy of princes," a source of pride in ownership and a way to get away from it all ("to the restless it always proves a remedy"). This rune does not appear among the Scandinavian runes. However, it is mentioned in one of the Cynewulfian signatures, short poetic riddles constructed on letters in the name of the poet Cynewulf, where he says "the horse measured the mile-long roads, the proud one raced in its filigreed trappings." The associations here are speed, pride, and beauty.

A horse from modern literature that well exemplifies the rune god Ehwaz is the stallion named Shadowfax that is ridden by the wizard Gandalf in J. R. R. Tolkien's fantasy epic *The Lord of the Rings*. Shadowfax understands the speech of men, is the swiftest and most graceful of all horses, and never grows tired. By day his coat is silver, but at night it is gray. He is too proud to bear a saddle, but will sometimes consent to let noble men and women ride him.

## Mannaz

This rune stands for the first man, the Teutonic Adam, created by Woden from an ash tree. The god of this rune is primordial man, the archetype of the human race who embodies the living spirit of the race, in much the same way that the spirit of a race of beasts is concentrated in the sacred white individuals that rarely appear on the Earth. In Hebrew folklore Adam is regarded as a divine hero or lesser god, who is more beautiful, longer of life, and wiser than his descendants because he is nearer to the source of creation.

In the Kabbalah, the mystical philosophy of the Jews, heavenly Adam is called Adam Kadmon. He is the Microprosopos or Lesser Countenance, in contrast to God the Father who is the Macroprosopos or Greater Countenance. Adam Kadmon is only slightly less powerful and holy than God. In fact he is God expressing himself through the human form. In Christianity heavenly man is represented by Jesus after his ascent to heaven. Christ is another form of Adam Kadmon. There is reason to suppose that Mannaz was regarded by the Teutons in much the same way that Adam was looked upon by the Hebrews.

In the *Icelandic Rune Poem* Mannaz seems to be symbolized by the phallus. At least, this is the impression I receive from the imagery. It is said to be "the joy of man" and an "augmentation of the dust/and adorner of ships." The joy of man may be sexual joy and pride in virility. Augmentation of the dust may refer here to the spilling of semen. The riddling remark that the rune is the adorner of ships is more difficult to understand, but the ships of the Vikings were always adorned with an up-thrusting prow in the shape of a dragon. The dragon is often identified with the serpent, and because of its shape the serpent is a universal symbol for the penis.

If Mannaz is translated simply as man, which is the usual practice, the first line of this stanza, "man is the joy of man," makes no sense. However, if the rune is translated as penis or erect sexual member, the line would read "virility is the joy of man," which does make sense. In the other two major rune poems Mannaz is described more literally as a mortal human being. The *Old English Rune Poem* inserts a tone of Christian misery that is completely foreign to the pagan spirit, saying "everyone must betray his fellow,/because the Lord purposes by his decree/to commit the wretched human body to the earth."

In my opinion, the meaning of erect phallus suggested by the *Icelandic Rune Poem* is closer to the original understanding of this rune. Masculine virility was looked upon as an expression of the creative spirit of humankind, the pride and strength of man, even the identity of man. For many men this attitude continues to be held today. Adam is before all else the father of the human race, an incarnated form of God, just as Mannaz is an incarnated form of the All-father, Woden. Secondary associations are the virtues specific to human beings, not shared by the beasts, such as intelligence, speech, and free will. The first man possesses these virtues to a greater degree than all the lesser men who follow him.

■ Literally "water," in the *Old English Rune Poem* it is the water of the sea that is intended. The imagery is very threatening. The sea is called "interminable" to those men who are "obliged to venture out in a tossing vessel," and the waves are said to "terrify them exceedingly." The ship, which is poetically compared with the horse because men ride it, "will not respond to the bridle."

The references in the other rune poems are to smaller inland bodies of water. In the *Icelandic Rune Poem* Laguz is described as "welling stream/and broad geyser/and land of the fish." In the *Norwegian Rune Poem* it is "where a cascade falls from a mountain side." The enigmatic riddle line is added, "but ornaments are made of gold." This suggests that water was regarded as beautiful and attractive but of no permanent value. Its beauty cannot be captured and shaped, as can the beauty of gold.

There are numerous folk tales in the north concerning men lured to their deaths by water nymphs who appear in the shapes of beautiful naked women. From the waist up they are human in appearance, but from the waist down they are often scaled and serpentine or fish-shaped. This symbolism arises from the association between water and the unconscious. What projects into the conscious awareness of the mind is known, but what remains hidden below the surface in the unconscious is unknown, and therefore dangerous and frightening.

The best-developed deity who fits this role of watery temptress is Ran (the Ravisher). She is the wife of the giant Aegir, and dwells with him in his incredibly rich palace beneath the waves of the sea. All the gold that has ever been lost by shipwreck rests in Aegir's palace. So great is the shining of the gold, the

giant has no need for torches to light his lavish feasts.
Ran owns a vast net with which she forever tries to
ensnare seafarers. It is she who stirs up the waves and
causes them to imperil ships. Those she drowns are
welcomed into her hall and served a fine fish dinner.
She has nine daughters who represent the waves. They
are temptresses, just like their mother, and drag men
they have bewitched with their beauty to the bottom
of the sea.

Water is seductive and treacherous, but also a source
of creativity and renewal. Many wonders lie hidden
beneath its surface. This rune should not be regarded as
wholly negative, but as possessing a mixture of good
and bad qualities. Another spirit of the waters is the
wise giant Mimir from whom Woden sought wisdom.
Mimir watches over the well of the waters of wisdom
that lies beneath one of the three roots of Yggdrasill. In
return for a drink of these waters, Woden gave Mimir
one of his eyes as a pledge. Because of this, Woden is
known as the One-eyed. Mimir may be regarded as the
god of the more benign aspects of Laguz.

## Inguz

This is one of the few runes that may be explicitly connected with a known god, Ing, the fertility god of the
East-Danes. This god has been linked with Freyr, and
probably shared many of the attributes of Freyr. Indeed,
they may be one and the same god—*freyr* literally
means "lord." The full title of this single god may be
*Yngvi-Freyr-inn-Frodi*, which translates to "Lord Yngvi
the Fruitful."[18]

Two beasts sacred to Freyr were the boar and the
horse. Freyr's horse was Freyfaxi ("Freyr's Maned-
One"). Both animals are symbols of virility and fertility. Ing is said in the *Old English Rune Poem* to be "first"

among the East-Danes, suggesting that the god was considered to be the founding father of the tribe. His statue was drawn in a ceremonial chariot on special occasions. The poet relates that the statue of the god, and later his chariot, were taken across the sea to the east, perhaps to eastern Sweden, or Svealand, for the purpose of increasing the fertility of herds or crops in that region.

Freyr was the bringer of peace and happiness. However, he had his dark side. As a fertility god, human sacrifices were offered to him once a year in Sweden at the festival of the *Froblod* ("Freyr's Sacrifice"). Sacrifices were also conducted by the Sons of Freyr, the Ynglingar, in Uppsala. Sexual practices accompanied his rituals. These are described as "an unmanly clatter of bells and effeminate gestures."[19] Possibly his male worshipers were offering themselves as symbolic brides to the god. One of his statues is in the form of a male figure with a gigantic phallus.

## Dagaz

This rune means light of day. In the *Old English Rune Poem* it is said to be "sent by the Lord, beloved by mankind," and is "the glorious light of the Creator," a source of joy and hope that shines down on the powerful and powerless with equal benefit. There may be a Christian influence in this description, but it probably is based on an older pagan concept of daylight as the gift of the Sun god to all of humanity. The Sun was worshiped in very early times in the form of a golden solar disk that was drawn along during ceremonial processions in a ritual chariot.

This rune, the light of the Sun or daylight, is connected with Sowelu, the Sun itself or more specifically the rays from the Sun. Since Thor was a sky god who battled the forces of chaos with thunderbolts, it would not be unreasonable to connect him with Dagaz as well as with Sowelu. However, for the sake of distinction between these two runes it might be better to conceive the god in the guise of the Alcis, twin deities worshiped by the Germans who were identified by the Romans with Castor and Pollux. They, or deities very much like them, appear on the Tarot card The Sun in the Marseilles deck. They are shown on the card as naked or nearly naked golden-haired twin boys around nine years old who stand together in front of a brick wall beneath a rain of Sun-drops.

## Othila

This is the rune for homeland. It is mainly positive in the *Old English Rune Poem*, with only a minor cautionary note interjected by the poet. He calls the family land "dear to every man" provided that he is able to enjoy within the walls of his own house "everything that is right and proper in constant prosperity." The implication is that when a human being is not permitted to act freely and prosper within his or her own land, the joyful association vanishes.

This rune is also related to the grave, the final homeland of every mortal. In the end it is only the land where our corpse lies that we actually possess; indeed, it is only the dust from which our frail human bodies are made that is truly our native soil. Everything else can be taken from us in life, but only death can deprive us of this fleshy residence for our spirit. From a philosophical point of view, if we attain harmony within our own physical shell, we also attain harmony with the entire universe no matter how much or how little property we possess; if we are in discord with our own nature, we are in discord with all the world.

The rune god of Othila will differ from person to person. It is the deity that most perfectly represents the cultural or racial identity of an individual. It may be a tribal god, the personification of a nation such as the goddess America, or the tutelary god of a specific sect, clan, or family. In ancient times families had their own personal deities, represented by small statues, that were kept inside the house and served at it guardian spirits. These household gods protected all the inhabitants of the house who paid them regular worship.

It was common in past ages for specific places such as groves, hills, springs, streams, rivers, valleys, and villages to have their own tutelary gods or goddesses. These deities were worshiped in the places sacred to them, and offered protection, healing and divination to human beings who paid them worship and made sacrifices to them. Often temples or towns grew up in such sacred spots to surround the dwelling place of the god or goddess. If you happen to know the name of the deity of the place where you live, and you feel a deep attachment to that place, this deity will be your rune god of Othila.

# Quick Reference Guide

## Runes

### 1. Fehu (Feoh): *f*
**Literal:** Cattle.
**Abstract:** Possessions, ownership, wealth, submissiveness, slavery.

### 2. Uruz (Ur): *u*
**Literal:** Aurochs, an extinct type of wild ox.
**Abstract:** Virility, freedom, courage, manhood, test of strength, power, the will.

### 3. Thurisaz (Thorn): *th*
**Literal:** A devil or evil giant.
**Abstract:** Malice, wickedness, vengeance, hatred, spite, slanders, underhanded dealings, evil, the Devil.

## 4. Ansuz (Os): *a*

**Literal:** The wise god Woden.
**Abstract:** Wisdom, eloquence, persuasiveness, authority, ruling power, law-giver, magical knowledge, God.

## 5. Raido (Rad): *r*

**Literal:** Riding, a journey on horseback.
**Abstract:** Travel, a quest, seeking, exploration, communication.

## 6. Kano (Cen): *k, c, q*

**Literal:** A torch or beacon.
**Abstract:** Guiding star, object of a quest, holy grail, a guide or teacher, illumination on the path, truth, revelations.

## 7. Gebo (Gyfu): *g*

**Literal:** Gift or sacrifice.
**Abstract:** A present, a gift for service, an achievement, an avocation, a religious calling, an inherent talent, devotion, something given or received.

## 8. Wunjo (Wyn): *w, v*

**Literal:** Joy or glory.
**Abstract:** Ecstasy, heavenly blessings, rewards, recognition, fame, celebrity, renown, victory in contests and sports, titles bestowed.

## 9. Hagalaz (Haegl): *h*

**Literal:** Hail.
**Abstract:** Destruction, violence, loss, deprivation, a storm or other natural disaster, wrath, punishment, injury, fury, conflicts, an attack.

## 10. Nauthiz (Nyd): *n*

**Literal:** Necessity to endure.

**Abstract:** Suffering, hardship, pain, need for endurance, survival, last resource of strength called upon, torture, servitude.

## 11. Isa (Is): *i*

**Literal:** Ice.

**Abstract:** Coldness, a hard heart, fascination, allure, enticement, entrapment, deception, false appearances, cessation of progress, an enchantress.

## 12. Jera (Ger): *j*

**Literal:** Harvest season, year.

**Abstract:** End of a cycle, turn of the wheel, change, reversal of fortune, reaping what has been sown, fulfillment, completion, new beginnings.

## 13. Eihwaz (Eoh): *y*

**Literal:** Yew.

**Abstract:** Resilient strength, dependability, a trustworthy companion, magical power, commanding occult forces.

## 14. Perth (Peordh): *p*

**Literal:** Apple.

**Abstract:** Luxury, pleasure, sensuality, enjoyment of life, over-indulgence, intoxication, gaming, gambling, divination.

## 15. Algiz (Eolh): *z, x*

**Literal:** Defense.

**Abstract:** Warding off of danger, protective

amulet or symbol, taboo, barrier, shield, armor, averting of evil, a defender.

## 16. Sowelu (Sigel): s

**Literal:** Lightning or solar ray.

**Abstract:** Fire from the heavens, divine intervention, an omen or portent, righteous wrath of God, punishment for sin or the violation of laws, sword of retribution, judgment, justice, fulfillment of karma.

## 17. Teiwaz (Tir): t

**Literal:** Tew, god of oaths and battle.

**Abstract:** Courage, war skills, weapons, strength in battle, honor, nobility of purpose, strong principles, promises, oaths, pledges, contracts, legal matters.

## 18. Berkana (Beorc): b

**Literal:** Birch.

**Abstract:** Sexuality, desire, love-making and lovers, virility, fertility, conception, new life, new growth, awakenings, beginning of change, renewal, birth of children.

## 19. Ehwaz (Eoh): e

**Literal:** Horse.

**Abstract:** Means to an end, conveyance, vehicle, instrument, tool, machine, swiftness, physical strength, physical grace, physical beauty, the human body.

## 20. Mannaz (Man): *m*

**Literal:** Man.

**Abstract:** Adam the first human, the microcosm, the soul, intelligence, the way or method to an end, solution to a problem, cleverness, the magician, the trickster, mental strength, mental virtues, mental graces, the human mind.

## 21. Laguz (Lagu): *l*

**Literal:** Water.

**Abstract:** The unconscious, the womb, dreams, fantasies, hopes, physical appearance, beauty, vanity, fashions, fads, impermanent things, fickleness, changeability, adaptability.

## 22. Inguz (Ing): *ng*

**Literal:** Fertility god.

**Abstract:** The home, the hearth, the family, father, nurture, growth, development, evolution, homely virtues, basic decency and humanity.

## 23. Dagaz (Daeg): *d*

**Literal:** Daylight.

**Abstract:** Clarity, understanding, perception, openness, enlightenment, completeness, a totality, wholeness, harmony.

## 24. Othila (Ethel): *o*

**Literal:** Native land.

**Abstract:** Homeland, place of birth, roots, culture, tribe, race, nation, sense of identity, name, house and land, the grave.

# The Aettir

**Fehu Aett**
Fixed (the past).

**Hagalaz Aett**
Mutable (the present).

**Teiwaz Aett**
Cardinal (the future).

# The Pairs

**Fehu-Uruz**
Subservience-freedom.

**Thurisaz-Ansuz**
Evil-good.

**Raido-Kano**
Quest-beacon.

**Gebo-Wunjo**
Sacrifice-glory.

**Hagalaz-Nauthiz**
Violence-endurance.

**Isa-Jera**
Stillness-change.

**Eihwaz-Perth**
Vitality-sensuality.

**Algiz-Sowelu**
Protection-punishment.

**Teiwaz-Berkana**
Fighting-loving.

**Ehwaz-Mannaz**
Means-method.

**Laguz-Inguz**
Fantasy-practicality.

**Dagaz-Othila**
Completeness-identity.

# Interpreting the Runes

## Distance from the Diviner

**Nearest Rune**—Past or foundation of the matter.

**Middle Two Runes**—Present or near future.

**Farthest Rune**—Distant future or resolution of the matter.

**Equal Distance**—Runes act at the same time.

## Separation of Runes

**Regular Spacing**—Events surrounding the question unfold smoothly and gradually.

**Gaps**—Time of waiting.

**Clumping**—Events happen together.

- **Three runes left, one right:** Private matters, inner or psychological events, the querent is the observer or reactor.

- **One rune left, three runes right:** Public matters, outer or physical events, querent is the prime mover of events.

- **Three runes close, one rune far:** Immediate resolution of the matter, with some unforeseen event in the future.

- **One rune close, three runes far:** Immediate event that will cause important repercussions in the future.

**Contact (within one dimension of the dice)**—Runes must be considered together.

- **Two runes touching:** Lovers, friends, married couple, important meeting with an individual.

- **Three runes touching:** Child, family, small gathering.

- **Four runes touching:** Large social gathering, important event.

## Position of Runes

Nearest—Past, foundation.

Farthest—Future, outcome.

Left—Hidden, unconscious, mental, reception, something done to the querent.

Right—Known, conscious, physical, projection, something done by the querent.

Center—Events of pivotal importance

## Rune Patterns

Lines—Runes act by cause and effect as links in a chain.

Curves—Direction the curve bends is an attracting influence on runes in the curve.

- **Bend downward:** past influence.
- **Bend upward:** future influence.
- **Bend left:** hidden or unconscious influence.
- **Bend right:** revealed or physical influence.

Zigzags—Abrupt and unexpected changes.

Triangle—Happy figure; harmonious action of the constituent runes.

- **Fourth rune opposite side (base) of triangle:** Foundation.
- **Fourth rune opposite point (apex) of triangle:** Resolution.
- **Fourth rune inside triangle:** The querent.

## Polarities

Positive—Active, spontaneous, expressive.

Negative—Passive, reactive, repressive

## Qualities

Cardinal—Assertive, enterprising, outgoing.

Mutable—Changeable, adaptable, versatile.

Fixed—Steadfast, intense, focused.

## Elements

Fire—Energetic, forceful, expansive.

Water—Emotional, impressionable, intuitive.

Air—Communicative, witty, restless.

Earth—Practical, enduring, self-restrained.

## Planets

Moon—Rhythms, instincts, habits.

Mercury—Eloquence, invention, cunning.

Venus—Affection, sensitivity, sympathy.

Sun—Wholeness, identity, integration.

Mars—Aggression, self-assertion, passion.

Jupiter—Expansion, growth, joviality.

Saturn—Restriction, self-discipline, rigidity.

Aries—Cardinal-Fire; Positive.
> Outward-looking, enterprising, energetic, assertive.

First House—The querent, personal interests, hobbies.

Taurus—Fixed-Earth; Negative.
> Practical, productive, enduring, methodical.

Second House—Money, possessions, strong feelings.

Gemini—Mutable-Air; Positive.
> Communicative, adaptable, spontaneous, variable.

Third House—Communications, visits, brothers or sisters.

Cancer—Cardinal-Water; Negative.
> Sensitive, protective, nurturing, intuitive.

Fourth House—The mother, the home, the womb.

Leo—Fixed-Fire; Positive.
> Powerful, impressive, controlling, self-assured.

Fifth House—The father, creativity, pleasures.

Virgo—Mutable-Earth; Negative.
> Critical, analytical, efficient, modest.

Sixth House—Work, service, health.

Libra—Cardinal-Air; Positive.
> Diplomatic, idealistic, indecisive, easy-going.

Seventh House—Husband or wife, partner, close friend.

Scorpio—Fixed-Water; Negative.
> Intense, penetrating, secretive, sexual.

Eighth House—Legacies, occult experiences, death.

**Sagittarius**—Mutable-Fire; Positive.

Far-ranging, exploring, freedom-loving, adventurous.

**Ninth House**—Travel, foreign lands, visionary schemes.

**Capricorn**—Cardinal-Earth; Negative.

Disciplined, rational, prudent, serious.

**Tenth House**—Career, occupation, responsibilities.

**Aquarius**—Fixed-Air; Positive.

Emotionally detached, unconventional, reformist, rebellious.

**Eleventh House**—Acquaintances, social groups, organizations.

**Pisces**—Mutable-Water; Negative.

Intuitive, impressionable, sympathetic, submissive.

**Twelfth House**—Hidden matters, self-sacrifice, the unconscious.

# NOTES

■——————— Chapter Four

1. Pausanias. *Guide to Greece* 7.25.6. Translated by Peter Levi. Two volumes (Harmondsworth: Penguin, 1971), Vol. 1, 298–9.

2. Agrippa, Henry Cornelius. *Three Books of Occult Philosophy* 3.52. Edited and annotated by Donald Tyson (St. Paul: Llewellyn Publications, 1993), 636.

3. Plato. *The Phaedrus* 274c. *The Collected Dialogues*. Edith Hamilton and Huntington Cairns, editors (Princeton: Princeton University Press, 1973), 520.

4. *Sepher Yetzirah*, Chapter I. Translated by W. Wynn Westcott (New York: Samuel Weiser, 1980), 17.

5. See Meric Casaubon, *A True and Faithful Relation* (London: 1659), 355–6, for a proof that the Enochian Watchtowers are to be conceived as the sides of a cube. Aleister Crowley recognized the

necessity for this cubic model of the Watchtowers—see the autobiographical *Confessions of Aleister Crowley*, edited by John Symonds and Kenneth Grant (London: Penguin Books, 1989), 612.

## Chapter Nine

6. See *Tetragrammaton: The Secret to Evoking Angelic Powers and the Key to the Apocalypse* by Donald Tyson (St. Paul: Llewellyn Publications, 1995), 13–29, for a full examination of the significance of three and four in IHVH.

## Chapter Thirteen

7. Shakespeare, William. *As You Like It*, Act 2, Scene 7, lines 143–66.

8. Ptolemy. *Tetrabiblos*. Book IV, Chapter 10.

9. Tyson, Donald. *New Millennium Magic* (St. Paul: Llewellyn Publications, 1996), Chapter 33. The explanation and justification for this system of planetary colors also occurs in Chapter 33 of the original version of this work, *The New Magus*.

## Chapter Fifteen

10. Tyson, Donald. *Rune Magic* (St. Paul: Llewellyn Publications, 1988), 168–70.

11. Ibid., 34.

12. Ibid., 33.

13. Ibid., 32.

14. Ibid., 36.

15. Elliott, Ralph W. V. *Runes: An Introduction* (Manchester: Manchester University Press, 1959), 68.

16. This technique is briefly but clearly described in Israel Regardie's *The Golden Dawn* (St. Paul: Llewellyn Publications, 1990), sixth edition, 487. The technique of vibration is treated more extensively in Chapter VI of my book *Tetragrammaton*.

17. Book of Genesis, 9:3–5.

## Chapter Eighteen

18. Turville-Petre, E. O. G. *Myth and Religion of the North: The Religion of Ancient Scandinavia* (London: Weidenfeld and Nicolson, 1964), 170.

19. Ibid., 174.

# BIBLIOGRAPHY

■——Alexander, Michael (translator). *The Earliest English Poems*. Harmondsworth, Middlesex: Penguin Books Limited, 1966.

Blum, Ralph. *The Book of Runes*. Agincourt, Ontario: Methuen, 1982.

Church, Alfred John and William Jackson Brodribb (translators). *The Complete Works of Tacitus*. New York: Random House, Inc., 1942.

Cooper, D. Jason. *Esoteric Rune Magic*. St. Paul: Llewellyn Publications, 1994.

Elliot, Ralph W. V. *Runes: An Introduction*. Manchester: Manchester University Press, 1959.

Fox, Denton and Hermann Palsson (translators). *Grettir's Saga*. Toronto: University of Toronto Press, 1974.

252

Gordon, R. K. (translator). *Anglo-Saxon Poetry*. London: J. M. Dent and Sons Ltd., 1926.

Halsall, Maureen. *The Old English Rune Poem: A Critical Edition*. Toronto: University of Toronto Press, 1981.

Handford, S. A. (translator). *Caesar: the Conquest of Gaul*. Harmondsworth, Middlesex: Penguin Books Limited, 1951.

Hatto, A. T. (translator). *The Nibelungenlied*. Harmondsworth, Middlesex: Penguin Books Limited, 1965.

Howard, Michael A. *The Runes and Other Magical Alphabets*. Wellingborough, Northamptonshire: The Aquarian Press Limited, 1981.

Johnston, George (translator). *The Saga of Gisli*. Toronto: University of Toronto Press, 1963.

Morris, William and Eirikr Magnusson (translators). *Volsunga Saga: The Story of the Volsungs and Niblungs, with Certain Songs from the Elder Edda*. London: Walter Scott, 1888.

Page, R. I. *Reading the Past: Runes*. Berkeley and Los Angeles: University of California Press, 1987.

Palsson, Hermann and Paul Edwards (translators). *Egil's Saga*. Harmondsworth, Middlesex: Penguin Books Ltd., 1976.

Spaeth, J. Duncan (translator). *Old English Poetry: Translations into Alliterative Verse with Introductions and Notes*. Princeton, New Jersey: Princeton University Press, 1927.

Thorsson, Edred. *Futhark: A Handbook of Rune Magic*. York Beach, Maine: Samuel Weiser, Inc., 1984.

Thorsson, Edred. *Northern Magic: Mysteries of the Norse, Germans & English*. St. Paul: Llewellyn Publications, 1992.

Thorsson, Edred. *Rune Might: Secret Practices of the German Rune Magicians*. St. Paul: Llewellyn Publications, 1989.

Thorsson, Edred. *Runelore*. York Beach, Maine: Samuel Weiser, Inc., 1987.

Turville-Petre, E. O. G. *Myth and Religion of the North: The Religion of Ancient Scandinavia*. London: Weidenfeld and Nicolson, 1964.

Tyson, Donald. *The Truth About Runes*. St. Paul: Llewellyn Publications, 1995.

———. *New Millenium Magic*. St. Paul: Llewellyn Publications, 1996.

———. *Rune Magic*. St. Paul: Llewellyn Publications, 1988.

———. *Rune Magic Cards*. St. Paul: Llewellyn Publications, 1988.

———. *Power of the Runes*. St. Paul: Llewellyn Publications, 1989.

Young, Jean I. *The Prose Edda of Snorri Sturluson: Tales From Norse Mythology*. Cambridge: Bowes & Bowes, 1954.

# Stay in Touch. . .

**Llewellyn publishes hundreds of books on your favorite subjects.**
On the following pages you will find listed some books now available on related subjects. Your local bookstore stocks most of these and will stock new Llewellyn titles as they become available. We urge your patronage.

## Order by Phone
Call toll-free within the U.S. and Canada, 1–800–THE MOON. In Minnesota call (612) 291–1970. We accept Visa, MasterCard, and American Express.

## Order by Mail
Send the full price of your order (MN residents add 7% sales tax) in U.S. funds to:

> Llewellyn Worldwide
> P.O. Box 64383, Dept. K-749-8
> St. Paul, MN 55164–0383, U.S.A.

## Postage and Handling
- $4.00 for orders $15.00 and under
- $5.00 for orders over $15.00
- No charge for orders over $100.00

We ship UPS in the continental United States. We cannot ship to P.O. boxes. Orders shipped to Alaska, Hawaii, Canada, Mexico, and Puerto Rico will be sent first-class mail.

International orders: Airmail—add freight equal to price of each book to the total price of order, plus $5.00 for each non-book item (audiotapes, etc.). Surface mail—Add $1.00 per item.

Allow 4–6 weeks delivery on all orders. Postage and handling rates subject to change.

## Group Discounts
We offer a 20% quantity discount to group leaders or agents. You must order a minimum of five copies of the same book to get our special quantity price.

## Free Catalog
Get a free copy of our color catalog, *New Worlds of Mind and Spirit*. Subscribe for just $10.00 in the United States and Canada ($20.00 overseas, first class mail). Many bookstores carry *New Worlds*—ask for it!